Table of Contents

Contents

Part One: Prelude

I took a little walk...

Expectations? None.

Hopes? Infinite.

I began walking May 21st, 2012 at the abbey of Montserrat near Barcelona in Catalunya. Destination: First, Santiago de Compostela, and then on to Finisterre on the Atlantic Ocean. One thousand, two-hundred fifty kilometers.

I had no idea what to expect. Looking back, I wish I could have foreseen the contentment, the joy, the absolute feeling of freedom and one-ness with everything I was to experience. I have no idea how knowing that would have changed anything. Probably, it wouldn't. But something inside me, for some reason, wants that I had known that I was about to experience the happiest fifty days of my life. It wasn't an easy journey: My flat, mis-shapen feet screamed in pain by the end of every day and my frustration at not having a sufficient command of Spanish, at not knowing the customs, of being forever a stranger in a strange land were constant thorns in my side. Being lost in the desert in Aragon, walking many days in heat of over 100 degrees with no shade to be found the entire day and on one occasion running out of water well before reaching a town where I could get more, trying to make sense of a guide written in Catalan, having blisters on top of blisters (I didn't even know that was possible), walking ten hours when my guidebook said the day's route should take seven. Through all that, still, without a doubt in my mind, I was happier during my Camino experience than I had ever been in my entire life. Truth to tell, I'm afraid that I'll never be that happy again.

I wrote this as a series of blog entries well after I'd returned to the States from Spain as a record of my thoughts and memories of that pilgrimage, trying to work through what I can only describe as a type of post-traumatic stress syndrome. Due to constant state of warfare and the concomitant focus on and worship of all things military in the United States, it's common knowledge now that people who go through horrific experiences often suffer from PTSD, finding it difficult to relate to "normal" life, to relate to other people, to feel connected with the society they are physically a part of. They may feel emotionally numb, have no interest in people and things they used to enjoy, they may feel tense or on-edge and have angry outbursts for no reason. Those were the symptoms I had after returning from the Camino, symptoms I can only attribute to having left something that was as far to the good extreme of the spectrum of human experience as warfare, the more common cause of PTSD, is to the bad. I wouldn't compare my PTSD with that of someone who has experienced the horrors of war or extreme tragic events, but that seems the best way to describe my emotional state that still lingers more than a year after I walked into Santiago de Compostela.

I plan to take another pilgrimage in the future, trying to recapture the happiness and contentment I experienced between Montserrat and Finisterre. On the next journey, do I expect to find the same emotional high that I experienced on the Camino de Santiago? No.

Do I hope for it? Infinitely so.

Esperando

Esperar: to wait: (Spanish) (verb, intransitive)

Esperar: to hope: (Spanish) (verb, intransitive)

The study of language is, for me, nothing short of fascinating. You can learn so much about a culture by how ideas are transmitted via sounds, words, and the grammar of the language; how subtle differences in meaning are expressed through the metaphors that are words and, when combined, become sentences, paragraphs, and the language of a people.

The verbs wait and hope, so different in English, curiously, are the same word in Spanish. This suggests people of Anglo descent, English speakers, find it possible, even normal, to wait without purpose, neither hoping, nor despairing. The Anglo can wait without hoping. Just as telling, he can hope without waiting. The two verbs need not cohabitate; they need not even be aware of the other's existence. We simply wait. The world passes by unnoticed, without anticipation, stoically, nonchalantly. We hope, *or* we wait.

How does a Hispanic person wait or hope? ¿Cómo espera el hispanohablante? With hope, con *esperanza*, with anticipation, looking forward to something better, *con felicidad* – with happiness. "*Mañana*" is a familiar word or expression to a *Norte Americano*. We use it synonymously with "later" and it usually carries with it a connotation of laziness and whatever is being put off until *mañana* isn't very important. But we misinterpret. The word is not void of anticipation. *Mañana* is not an empty promise which one simply waits for; it's pregnant. The Hispanic person doesn't wait without hope. There is anticipation. There is hope for improvement. A new day will dawn and with it, something that might bring us closer to something wonderful. Waiting is not lonely; it never arrives without its good friend, Hope. Hoping must entertain and be infinitely patient with its constant companion and true friend, Waiting. As surely as the Hispanic waits for *mañana*, hope is never far away. They both exist in the same space, at the same time, with divine anticipation thoroughly embedded in the waiting.

Forty-four years

I have had an inexplicable emotional tie to Spain for forty-four years. Or to put it more precisely, *he estado esperado desde hace cuarenta y quatro años*. I have been *waiting and hoping* since 44 years ago.

In early mid-life I met and had a ten-year intense relationship with a woman of Spanish heritage. (I believe now that any relationship with a Spanish woman is bound to be intense, but I didn't know that at the beginning of our relationship.) She took me with her on one of her frequent trips to Spain and the scales fell from my eyes. Amid the confusion, the noise, the rigidity, bureaucracy, and downright inefficiency of the culture, I fell in love with the country. Even now, many years later and after several trips to Spain, from Andalucía to Galicia, I cannot, for the life of me, explain what it is about that country that I love and that draws me back. It's something on a purely emotional and visceral level that defies description. But as the old beer commercial asked, why ask why?

Eight years

I waited eight years to walk the Camino de Santiago. I don't remember where or when I first heard about it but I have a memory of wanting to experience the pilgrimage that coincides with an event of eight years ago, so my pilgrimage to Santiago was at least that long in the making. I read web sites about it, read books about it, thought about it, planned it, bought supplies for it – everything but did it.

As a result of years of foolish decisions, bad luck, and just plain stupidity I had no savings. For most of my adult life, if I had lost my job I was at most two months from living on the streets. But there came a time when finally I had enough income over and above day to day living expenses that would allow me to pay off debt and put myself in a position of being able to leave my job, at least for the time required to walk the Camino. I didn't have any more savings than what was absolutely required to make the journey, and I still owed money on a car and a too-expensive Flamenco guitar I had recently purchased. (Remember the foolishness I mentioned above?) But I had enough in the bank to make minimum payments on those two debts, leave my job, and survive without income for several months. If my employer had offered an extended leave without pay I might have opted for that, but they didn't, sparing me that decision.

I was making a very good living and most people would have said I was foolish to leave. Well, being foolish isn't a foreign concept for me, and even today, being back in the "real world," having narrowly avoided financial disaster; I look back on the day I left my employer, seeing the office building in my rear view mirror, and vividly remember having admittedly mixed emotions: joy and happiness.

No regrets

March 16th, 2012. I had already sold everything I could and had given away almost all of the rest of my meager possessions. Some clothing, a backpack full of gear I'd need for the pilgrimage, a guitar, and a few bottles of wine (couldn't leave those; they didn't take much room anyway), and a few books I couldn't bear to part with were loaded in the car and I headed east from Seattle to spend a few weeks at my mother's house in Iowa before leaving for Spain. While there, I remodeled a room in her 130-year-old house and tried to wait patiently for my scheduled departure for Barcelona in May. I admit, I have every ounce of patience that God ever gave me because I've never used any of it. The wait was interminable, nearly impossible. I literally (and I don't use that word figuratively) counted the days to my departure.

With absolutely no idea what the next couple of months in Spain would bring, I felt like Tony in *West Side Story*:

> *Something's coming,*
> *don't know what it is,*
> *but I know it is*
> *gonna be great!*

Fortunately my older brother had a friend, a former painting student, in Barcelona who would let me crash at his apartment for a couple of days to catch up from jet lag before beginning my little walk across Spain. That was the only thing I could plan on. From that point forward all I knew was that I'd walk every day and figure it out, whatever "it" was, on a daily or hourly basis. I'd studied Spanish, mostly on my own, off and on for several years so I thought I'd be able to get by in a pinch, although I was soon to find out how weak my Spanish was even after all those years of studying. A language savant I am not.

I had read enough about the Camino to know that beginning at Montserrat was not the norm, and the route across Catalunya and Aragon was going to be lonely.

That was exactly what I wanted.

Sauntering

I came across an essay by Henry David Thoreau called *Walking*. Naturally, it caught my attention. Here is a paragraph from the first page:

> *I have met with but one or two persons in the course of my life who understand the art of Walking, that is, of taking walks – who had a genius, so to speak, for* SAUNTERING, *which word is beautifully derived "from idle people who roved about in the country, in the Middle Ages, and asked charity, under pretense of going* a la Sainte Terre," *to the Holy Land, till children exclaimed, "There goes a Saint-Terrer," a Saunterer, a Holy Lander. They who never go to the Holy Land in their walks, as they pretend, are indeed mere idlers and vagabonds; but they who do go there are saunterers in the good sense, such as I mean. Some, however, would derive the word from* sans terre, *without land or a home, which, therefore, in the good sense, will mean, having no particular home, but equally at home everywhere. For this is the secret of successful sauntering. He who sits still in a house all the time may be the greatest vagrant of all; but the saunterer, in the good sense, is no more vagrant that the meandering river, which is all the while sedulously seeking the shortest course to the sea.*

Imagine that. I was, for fifty days in 2012, in both senses of the word, a *saunterer*. I was on a holy, or spiritual, pilgrimage, following in the tradition of millions of people over the course of a thousand years, and I was also *sans terre* – I literally had no home. I had sold or given away virtually all my possessions and for the first time in my life had no address. When someone would ask me on the Camino where I lived I would tell them, honestly, that I had no home; I lived on the Camino. For fifty days, I was a free man, sauntering across Spain.

As I write this I'm trying to gather and order my feelings and memories so that I might convey some small sense of the freedom and happiness I experienced for that period of time walking across Northern Spain. I'm hoping that I'll find some words to help me coalesce my thoughts and emotions after the Camino, to help me find a place for them in my life "back in the world" where they might profit rather than haunt me as a type of phantom in my mind that continuously tries to draw me away from where I am – in the present, where I need to be now, fulfilling obligations and preparing for the next saunter – back to where I was, but which is just a place in memory that has come and gone and can't be relived.

Walking across Spain, for me, was therapeutic in the extreme. I felt these sentiments alternately and sometimes all at the same time:

• contentment with life, a life of no pressure to perform, to be anything other than who I was; to not be committed to anything other than taking another step;

• freedom from frustration of the working world and to simply enjoy each day, hour, and minute;

• happiness in small things – a small yellow arrow on the pavement that told me I was still on the Camino, ice cold beer and a *bocadillo* (sandwich) in the shade, a bar tender in an Irish bar who spoke English;

• joy when coming into a pueblo where I could sleep and rest my exhausted feet to prepare for another day;

• wonder at the life I observed in cities, towns, and tiny, ancient pueblos, all so completely and absolutely different from my life of 55 years in the United States;

• awe at the beauty of the countryside, the ancient architecture, the thought that generations of laborers and architects worked on even a small cathedral and that those at the beginning would never see the end; those at its completion would only have ghosts of ancestors to tell them of its beginning.

So I'll take another saunter, and it won't be the same. But I'll find more inspiration, more contentment, more happiness, more wonder, and more awe for the world. Of that I'm sure.

Part Two: Sauntering

Montserrat

May 20th

I left the apartment where I had stayed a couple of days in Barcelona at about 9:00 AM. Leaving earlier wouldn't have been a bad idea, but I didn't have an alarm and I was still not quite adjusted to Barcelona time. I purposefully left my watch, phone, computer, Kindle, everything possible that was electronic or electric at home. I wanted no semblance of the life I had left, a life in the world of schedules and phones and obligations. I did, however, bring an MP3 player/voice recorder, intending not to listen to it, but to record any thoughts I might have while walking so I wouldn't have to stop to write. Turns out, I'm not much of a talker and never used it to record a single thought. After about a month I changed my mind and began to occasionally listen to music as I walked, but that's a topic for a later chapter.

I had no earthly idea how to get to Montserrat from Barcelona, but that was part of the adventure. I had a guide to the city which listed a phone number for tourist information and after walking several blocks I was finally able to find a phone booth. How much money to deposit? I couldn't find any indication of the price of a local call on the phone or its kiosk, so I began putting the smallest coins I had in the slot until I got a dial tone and then dialed the number of the

Tourist Office, thankfully reaching an operator who spoke English. I can understand enough Spanish to talk with someone face-to-face and eventually comprehend what's being said after questions, clarifications, and restatements to ensure I understood what was said, but hearing and understanding through a telephone, dealing with street noise, and the absence of all visual cues from the other party in the conversation offers its own, sometimes insurmountable, challenges. Trying to get directions to the start of my pilgrimage, this was no time to challenge myself; I just wanted to get to the train station and on to Montserrat.

With directions and train numbers from the friendly and helpful woman on the other end of the line, I found the metro stop, boarded the right subway train, and was soon at *Espanya* Rail Station at *Plaça Espanya*. The train for Montserrat wasn't scheduled to leave for about an hour so I headed top side and wandered around until I found a *cafetería* where I had a very welcome *café con leche* and croissant, which would become my normal breakfast for the foreseeable future. It didn't take long to finish my coffee – no 16-ounce Starbucks lattes in Spain – so I quickly made my way back to the underground rail station, boarded the train, and made the uneventful and completely un-scenic trip to Monistrol, the small pueblo at the foot of the mountain on which sits the monastery of Montserrat. (The scenery between Barcelona and Monistrol might be described as Early Postmodern Industrial.)

I disembarked at the train station in Monistrol and asked directions to the center of town, figuring on a short walk from there to the monastery. I obviously hadn't done my homework. Had I stayed on the train, I would have been at Montserrat in another twenty minutes, much warmer and dryer, but, admittedly, without the sense of the accomplishment I was to experience some hours later after a grueling climb of over ten kilometers with a vertical ascent of 2,400 feet, some of it almost hand-over-hand climbing through rock and boulder-strewn landscape, through a thunderstorm and frigid winds, carrying twenty-five-pounds on my back. (Did I say I was having fun?) Yes, I had brought and was wearing a rain coat but I was as wet on the inside from perspiration as I was on the outside from the rain.

Arriving cold, wet, and sore, my first order of business was food and drink. This was the beginning of a wonderful time in my life, if for no other reason than I could eat and drink anything and everything I wanted and still lose weight. In fact, fast forward to about six weeks on the Camino and I had lost the twenty pounds I had been trying to lose unsuccessfully for many years; I was back to the same weight I had been when my son was born over twenty-five years earlier.

There is a modern cafeteria at Montserrat with every type of food anyone could want. I went right for the quarter roasted chicken, penne pasta, and a half bottle of *vino tinto de Rioja* (red wine from Rioja, a region I would walk through some weeks hence). It's the little things that make an impression on you while traveling and one of those things I absolutely love about Spain is that I never, not once, *nunca*, was asked for identification when I bought alcohol. I'm 55 years old and even if I want to flatter myself and say that I'm relatively young-looking – honestly, I don't look a day over 54 – it still irks me to get carded in the States when I buy alcohol. Zero tolerance, roughly translated, means zero brains.

But I digress.

After eating as much as I could – no problem with the half bottle of Rioja and pasta, but I admit I wasted some chicken – I began searching for the pilgrim's office where I would get my Pilgrim's Credentials, that fold-out card on which you receive a stamp of every pueblo or city in which you stay the night on the Camino to prove you've walked (or ridden, in the case of bicyclists and equestrians) the entire route. Some people have their credentials stamped at interesting sites they pass, at cathedrals, or other memorable places. It's a personal decision, but I only had mine stamped where I stopped for the night. (Coming in a future chapter: How I lost my pilgrim credential card, or better said, how it was stolen.) I registered as a Camino de Santiago pilgrim, received my credentials with the first stamp from the Monastery of Montserrat, and then was shown to the free *albergue* provided by the monastery. (A brief note of definition: an *albergue*, or *refugio*, is a place for pilgrims to stop to spend the night. They might be described as a bunk house; some very nice, most very basic, but all very welcome after a long day of walking. As millions of pilgrims have traveled a number of common routes from various points of origin throughout Spain and Europe, these albergues have been established at just about any city or pueblo a pilgrim might pass through. However, since the route beginning at Montserrat is relatively uncommon, the pilgrim won't find albergues in many of the pueblos along the Camino through Catalunya and Aragon. Until I reached Logroño, I stayed most nights in hostels and pensions.) As would be common for the part of the Camino between Montserrat and Logroño, I had the room to myself. In fact, in pueblos and cities where there was an albergue, until I got to Logroño, I would be the only guest. In this case, the albergue was divided into several rooms with three or four bunk beds in each. There was one other pilgrim there who also had his own room. He was on bicycle, so after we began the following morning I never saw him again.

After I got settled in my room, I went to the monastery book store. I had forgotten my guide to the Camino through Catalunya and Aragon and, silly me, thought I could just buy a guide at Montserrat. I wasn't so foolish to think I'd find a guide printed in English, but Spanish would be fine. *Sin problema*, I thought. There's bound to be a Camino de Santiago guide in Spanish here. I'm in Spain right?

Wrong. I was in Catalunya. The only guide available was in Catalan, and Catalan is NOT a dialect of what we refer to as Spanish, which is better described on the Iberian Peninsula as Castilian. I looked at the Catalan guide and quickly decided it would be almost useless to me. Not wanting to spend the money on something I could barely use, I figured I'd be able to find a Castilian language guide along the way. A very kind women at the pilgrim office found a Catalan guide with maps on the web and printed out enough pages to get me a few days down the road. I could barely understand it, but I could read the maps and it was better than nothing. That and those wonderful, lovely, magical yellow arrows got me to Lleída many days later where I finally found that guide in Castilian that I had been looking for. (Another note while I'm thinking of it – Lleída, the Catalan spelling for that city, is also known as Lerida in Castilian. I prefer to use the Catalan spelling because it's in Catalunya. It's their language, after all.)

I can't finish the recounting of my first day without a word about the Choir Boys and Monks of the Monastery at Montserrat. I embarked on the Camino de Santiago as a journey of spiritual reflection and discovery. There could have been no better way to begin than to attend Vespers at the cathedral and hear those voices. I cannot attempt to describe the music, just as I cannot even attempt to describe my emotional response to that event. Maybe a combination of the struggles I had been through to get to Montserrat, to get to the Camino after all these years, the waiting, the anticipation, the frustration I felt for so long at not being able to walk the Camino, then finally being there, experiencing the fulfillment of a dream of almost a decade, all combined with the visual impact of the cathedral, the aural impact of the voices, the spiritual impact of God's and my guardian angels' presence overwhelmed me to the point that a year later I still cannot talk of this experience. Even writing it is difficult. If my life had ended that night, after attending Vespers at the Cathedral at Montserrat, I would have died completely content, happy, and fulfilled. There were experiences yet to come on the Camino, some as powerful and life-changing as being present at vespers in the Cathedral of Montserrat, listening to those voices that night, but none more so.

The next morning I set out on a little walk that was to change my life.

Inside the Cathedral of Montserrat

Castellolí

May 21st

The first thing I wrote in my journal on the first day on the Camino was, "What a day!" When I wrote that I had stopped for lunch and didn't know it at the time, but I hadn't even half completed that day's walk. I stopped at a hotel-restaurant for a lunch of fried eggs, a pork chop, fried potatoes, (we call them French fries in the States) and a couple of glasses of wine. (I was in Spain after all.) Later on as the weather turned unbearably hot I'd switch to cold beer, served at a temperature of three degrees (centigrade), the tap icing over, but this day's walk had been through a cold wind, mostly on a highway, without knowing for most of the day if I was even on the right path. My Catalan guide, a few printed pages from the web, kindly given me by a person at the monastery, wasn't of much help and the yellow arrows of the Camino that would be so common later on were almost non-existent that first day. I can still remember distinctly, more than seven months later as I write this, the joy and relief I felt as I saw each yellow arrow that day, when I could find one, telling me that I was not lost in Catalunya.

I left the restaurant, rested, well fed, but at this point, completely lost. No yellow arrow, no indication in the guide of which direction to go (not that I could understand, anyway) and nothing but a busy interstate highway intersection ahead of me to try to circumnavigate. I found my way to a tiny, desolate pueblo near the intersection and walked up and down the streets, hoping to find someone who could point me in the right direction. No easy task, that, but I finally happened upon a man coming out of an apartment building and did my best to explain to him that I was making a pilgrimage to Santiago and couldn't figure out where to go next. He seemed very helpful, giving me directions to where I would find the Camino and I followed his directions to a T. Some hours later I figured out that this helpful gentleman must have thought I was making my way to Montserrat, whence I had come, which is another common pilgrim destination. (In fact, I had met a French man making that pilgrimage just a couple of hours earlier and had a very pleasant conversation with him, receiving many helpful tips for my own journey.) The man in the little pueblo had pointed me in the wrong direction and as I tried to follow my guide in combination with his directions I made a loop of maybe six or seven kilometers over a couple of hours, ending, sadly, at the restaurant at which I had eaten lunch earlier. Trying to look on the bright side, I had passed through a park-like area with historical markers from the Napoleonic wars between France and Spain in the early 1800's. Being a student of history, I have to admit that I enjoyed the little detour for that reason, although my feet, by this time, were in violent disagreement.

Much to my amazement, in the interim while I had been wandering through historical battle grounds, someone had painted a yellow arrow on the road right in front of the restaurant which pointed me in the right direction and I was able to continue on my way, sure in the knowledge that Santiago lay ahead, somewhere, someday.

My guide said that there was an albergue in Castellolí and I was even able to read its address. I was pretty sure that I understood enough of the Catalan guide to at least read a street name and number and I easily found the street in the tiny pueblo of Castellolí. Finally, upon reaching the numbered house, I rang the bell. A voice of an elderly woman answered on the intercom, and I announced, with exhaustion in my voice, that I was a pilgrim on the Camino de Santiago looking for the albergue and asked if this was it. (OK, my Spanish was a trifle more rudimentary. I think I said, "Is this an albergue?") The voice on the other side of the intercom said, "No." I heard a click and that was the end of the conversation.

Somewhat tired, sad, dejected, tired, frustrated, and tired, I looked around for someone of whom I could ask directions. My efforts were fruitless. I continued walking to the next pueblo, another kilometer down the road. The guide in my hands mentioned its name but the context of the sentence was lost on me. I arrived there and found it was basically a wide spot in the road. No albergue, no pension, no hostel, nothing, *nada*. I considered breaking out my tent and sleeping in a field but I happened upon a woman who told me that that was not allowed. She also told me, with great conviction on her part, that there was no albergue in Castellolí. Back to sad, tired, dejected, tired, frustrated and, (did I already mention?), tired. I walked up the street to a restaurant which was closed. (Naturally, I thought. My attitude was beginning to suffer just a little by this time.) But I saw someone inside and knocked on the door anyway. Doing my best to explain my situation and showing the kind gentleman the guide I was trying to follow, he told me that there was indeed an albergue in Castellolí, and told me where to find the bar at which someone would be able to give me a key to it. (A better English translation for the establishment would be "cafe." But they're called "bars" in Spain, so that's good enough for me.)

This was my first educational experience on the Camino Catalan: There are so few pilgrims on this particular route that the albergues, when they exist, are locked up, only open on an as-needed basis, and the pilgrim has to go to the town hall, the *Ayuntamiento*, to register, receive a stamp in his pilgrim credentials, and get a key to the albergue, which may or may not be close by. In Castellolí, because the *Ayuntamiento* was closed at this time of the day, I would find someone in the bar next door who would be able to help me. I walked the kilometer back to Castellolí, found the bar, and within it, a number of very friendly and helpful people. The key to the albergue was with someone who was not at the bar at present, but thankfully, reachable via cell phone, whom the bar manager called. She showed up a half hour later with the key, during which time, and more, I thoroughly enjoyed a simple dinner, a beer or two, and pleasant conversation with the regulars in the bar. After dinner I was shown across the street to a room in an unused school building, where I had an entire classroom floor and student bathroom to myself. This was the albergue. There was no shower, no hot water, and no bed, but I had completed my first day on the Camino, asking and receiving directions in Spanish (unsuccessfully in one case, as it turned out), finding my way to the first way-point, uninjured (save for a few blisters on the feet), fed, housed, exhausted, and elated.

Igualada

Although I was sleeping on a cold, hard, tile floor in a school room in Castellolí behind a wall of windows looking out on the main street of town, I had no trouble sleeping past 9:00 that morning. I had brought a one-man tent just in case I had the opportunity, or might be required to sleep outside. I also had an inflatable mattress that allowed a good night's sleep even on a hard school-room floor. I had pitched the tent in the school room to give myself some privacy as I slept. I felt as though I were on display for everyone to gawk at as they walked or drove by. However, the albergue was free and I wasn't complaining.

I had taken time to care for my blistered feet the night before, using plenty of Neosporin, gauze, and bandages, and redressed them that morning as I prepared for another day on the Camino. It would be a long time before dressing and redressing blisters would not be a twice-daily, sometimes thrice-daily routine. In the beginning I would stop mid-day either at a bar (with outside seating, of course) or just sit by the side of the road and dress new blisters. (As I got to the part of the Camino where there were more pilgrims I would sometimes notice signs in bars saying, "No bare feet!" Removing shoes and socks mid-day, especially when the

30

weather turned much warmer, was a common occurrence.) I had brought a first aid kit with what I thought were way too many Band-Aids and gauze pads. Fool that I was! I made three or four trips to the farmácia over the course of my weeks on the Camino to replenish my stores. I didn't use them all myself: Because I had the supplies, I became the foot doctor to a few people along the way. I wasn't the only one with blistered feet.

In my defense, it's not as though I was completely unprepared for the walk. I had bought the best-fitting boots I could find; price was no object. But my feet are not shaped normally–the arches are flat and my feet are too long from arch to toe in relation to the length from arch to heel, the heel is relatively narrow and the forefoot is wide, so shoes and boots never fit well. The fallen arches cause a general pain throughout the entire sole of my foot after about four to five hours of walking, and because of the unusual proportions of heel-to-arch and arch-to-toe, shoes either fit in the heel or the toe, but not both. For normal wear I can get by with a few brands of shoes that I've found over the years that give an adequate fit. (Born and Reebok are my favorites.) But for a trip of forty-eight days of walking, averaging a little over twenty-six kilometers a day, adequate wasn't nearly good enough. I had taken many long hikes on weekends before leaving for the Camino to prepare myself physically and break in my boots. And, for a fifty-five-year-old I'm fairly fit. But the constant, daily walking, normally covering from twenty-five to thirty-five kilometers daily, without time for my feet to recover, caused problems I didn't foresee.

But enough about that. St. Paul had his "thorn in the side" too. We don't know what that term referred to in his case, but with all the walking he did I'm inclined to believe that he had poor-fitting sandals and flat feet. And look at all the kilometers he covered without daily mid-day stops for a sandwich and a beer (or two). So, no more complaining from your humble narrator.

I finally got myself washed (in a stainless steel sink with cold and cold running water), dressed and packed, and then I headed over to the office of the *ayuntamiento* to turn in the key to the school, following which I went back to the bar where I had stopped for dinner the day before to have a *café con leche* and a croissant. The woman who was working there that morning, Carmen, was very friendly and even more talkative. I didn't leave until 11:30. I knew I had a very short day – Igualada, the next stop on the Camino being not too far away – and I enjoyed the opportunity to chat and practice my Spanish. Allowing my feet a few more hours of rest didn't seem like a bad idea either. Since I couldn't understand my Catalan guide very well, I asked Carmen how to get to Igualada, not thinking that I should have specified that I wanted to walk the Camino route to that town. Carmen gave me directions as if I were driving there, which I followed and ended up walking along a major highway all that afternoon and entering Igualada, not a small town, having no idea where to find the *Ayuntamiento*.

But the Camino gives everyone what he needs when he needs it, including information on where the *Ayuntamiento* is. I stopped at a restaurant for a glass of wine and easily got directions. (Did I mention how nice it is to be able to eat and drink all you want and still lose weight on the Camino?) I arrived at the *Ayuntamiento* at about 4:00, got my pilgrim passport stamped, and received further directions to a senior residence where I would receive the keys and then further directions, finally, to the albergue. (I was beginning to feel as if I were on a scavenger hunt.) This is how it works in Catalunyan and Aragonese pueblos where there actually are albergues: You first find the *Ayuntamiento*, check in to let the town constable know you're there, and then you are shown or given directions to the albergue or to where you can get the keys to it. I should mention here as a matter of information for future pilgrims who may be reading this that, while albergues are not the norm across Catalunya and Aragón, where they exist they are normally provided without charge. Even better, the town residents you meet at the *Ayuntamientos,* albergues, and bars seem to be very appreciative of the pilgrim traffic they receive and are for the most part more welcoming than you could possibly imagine.

I finally arrived at a very nice little building on the grounds of an old tannery, let myself in, disgorged my backpack on a table in a common area and chose my bed from among all of the rooms and beds in the albergue. Yet again, I had the entire place to myself.

After a shower and the daily foot dressing I headed to the center of town to get a bite to eat.

But first, a little observation:

Prior to leaving for Spain some people would ask me if I thought this might not be a good time to go there, given the political strife caused by the poor economics. My reply was, "A short life and a merry one, I always say!" But seriously, I wasn't really concerned. I might be completely naive, but it seems to me that a person can go to all but the most war-torn locations of the world without having to be overly fearful. There might be a few protests going on in the larger cities of Spain, but those were not my destination. Even if I were going to Madrid and planning to visit the *Plaza del Sol*, where, if there were going to be a demonstration, it would most certainly take place, I'd simply rearrange my visit for another day or bypass that location, finding someplace else to enjoy.

All that is to say, I headed down to Igualada's *Plaza Mayor* for dinner and what do you think I saw? Correctamundo! A political protest. But it was peaceful. There might have been two-hundred people in the square, and a few of them made speeches through a shared bull horn. Of course, I understood nothing. I asked a couple of policemen who were standing nearby what the protest was about. They told me that the people were protesting proposed cuts in social welfare benefits currently being discussed in Parliament. Hmmm. The country is broke and people are up in arms about the politicians discussing cuts in spending. That's why I ignore politics. Makes no sense at all to me. In fact, one of my fondest memories, rather, I should say lack of memories, is the complete absence of American politics during the entire time I was in Spain. Later, when I was in Granada, in a bar where there was a television, I saw something on the news that mentioned the American presidential race and I realized that that was the first time I had heard the names Obama and Romney since leaving the States in May.

I count that as one of the greatest blessings of the Camino.

My own private albergue in Igualada

Castellnou de Seana

May 24th

Looking through my journal to remind myself of what I did and felt each day, I find the next entry says, "*What day is it today? I don't know. I know it's Saturday – I found that out talking with the receptionist at the hotel but the date is a mystery. I've stopped in Lleída an extra day to rest. My left foot isn't well – swollen with blisters. But, I'm enjoying the trip.*

"*No one said it would be easy.*"

I've since looked at a map of my route and calculated that that must have been May 24th. I hadn't written anything since Igualada because at the end of the previous three days my remaining energy only allowed me to get something to eat, care for my feet, climb into bed, and sleep. I didn't write anything about the day I got to Castellnou de Seana, but I can still remember, many months later, how well I was treated there. I limped into the pueblo at about 7:00 PM – very late by pilgrim standards – because I slept late that morning and walked so slowly on my battered, camino-weary feet. By that time of day, of course, the *Ayuntamiento* was closed. I did the usual, though, asking whomever I could find where I might check in as a pilgrim and get help in finding the albergue. I could tell from my guide, a few pages printed from the web, that there was indeed an albergue in this town, so it was just a matter of finding it and being let in.

I was instructed by a couple of gentlemen sitting in front of the *Ayuntamiento* to go down the street to Café Modern. They said someone there would be able to help me. I hobbled down the street, maybe the length of two normal U.S. city blocks but seeming like another two kilometers, and found the café on the left. Entering it, I was greeted by a woman behind the counter at the far end of what was a large café by Spanish standards. If you've been with me this far, it goes without saying that the first thing I did upon unburdening my exhausted body of my back pack was to order a large, frigid beer. By this time in my journey the weather had "warmed" substantially. I say "warmed" because there's no such word as "hotted," although there should be just for this occasion. Afternoon temperatures were around one hundred degrees Fahrenheit with no shade available anywhere. Before leaving the States I had looked for a hat at an expensive outdoor equipment store, and found the prices more than a little unreasonable for a simple baseball cap. No problem, I thought, I'll get a hat in Spain. By the time I found a store where I could buy a hat on the Camino my balding head was the color of a stove coil on high and felt it, especially when I'd take a warm shower. (Why is it that, even after walking all day in the Mediterranean heat and sun of Spain, a warm shower still feels good?)

Anyway, back to the Café Modern. After ordering a *cerveza grande* I explained that a couple of gentlemen near the office of the *Ayuntamiento* told me that someone at this café might be able to help me check in to the albergue. The angel behind the bar said that that was indeed the case and she called the *alcalde*, the mayor, for me and explained to him that there was a pilgrim in town who would need the albergue for the night. After she hung up she told me that the *alcalde* would be at the *Ayuntamiento* in a few minutes to register me and give me the key to the albergue. In the meantime she would make dinner for me and she asked what I would like to eat. After a long, long, long, hot, hot, hot day of walking on my painful, fallen arches and feeling every old blister and each new blister as it formed on my feet, I thought I'd ended up in Mayberry and Aunt Bee was there to take care of me, a cool, damp cloth in one hand and a tall glass of sweet tea in the other. (I don't think Aunt Bee would ever serve beer: her one failing.) I thought I had died and gone to heaven. I think this was the first of uncountable instances on the Camino when the graciousness of the Spanish people in each Pueblo and all the other pilgrims I met along the way, and the little miracles that seemed to just keep happening overwhelmed me. Suddenly I wasn't tired, my feet didn't hurt, the air wasn't hot, and the feeling of the grace of God descending on me was as real as the sweating glass of beer in front of me. (Comparing God and beer when you've just completed a long, very hot day on the Camino is <u>not</u> sacrilege, I'm sure.)

A dear friend I was to meet later in Logroño gave me a card on which was a Pilgrim's Prayer, part of which asks God to be:

- The guide on our intersections;
- The strengthening during fatigue;
- The shadow in our heat;
- The consolation during dejection;
- And the power of our intention.

Whether it's God, our Guardian Angels, Jesus, Mary, St. James (Santiago), or their manifestations in the people we meet along the way, I don't know. But the fact that we pilgrims have a guide, the strength, shade from the sun, the consolation and the power that we need when we're most in need is obvious, even conspicuous every day on the Camino, and all were given to me at the Café Modern that afternoon in Castellnou de Seana.

I walked back to the *Ayuntamiento* and, presently, a man in an old Nissan pickup pulled up next to the building, introduced himself, and unlocked the door. Wearing my backpack, I wearily climbed the stairs to the third-floor office and signed the registry. Then he stamped my pilgrim passport with the town's official unique stamp, gave me a key, and drove me to the albergue some blocks away. Yet again, I was the only pilgrim in a modern, comfortable little bunk house. I showered, changed my clothes, and doctored my feet before returning to the Café Modern, where, after a few minutes I was served a large salad and spaghetti and meatballs that I had asked for earlier. It was as though I were an honored guest. While I was eating, the owner's son joined me and we had a pleasant conversation about the pueblo, the economy, the pilgrimage, and I forget what else. He brought out a pilgrim guestbook and invited me to add my comments, which I did, and then read other pilgrims' comments from days, weeks, months, and years past. It seems the treatment I received wasn't at all unusual in Castellnou de Seana.

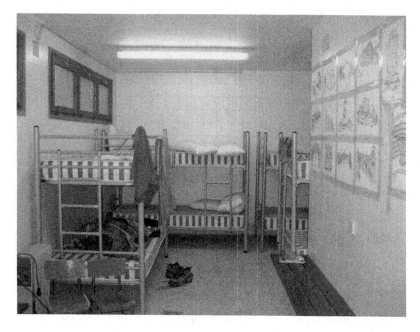

The albergue in Castellnou de Seana

Lleída

May 25th

Lleída – the largest city on my Camino since leaving Barcelona. I limped into the city, almost crawling; my feet had walked their last kilometer. Every step for the last hour or more had been one more than I thought I could possibly take. I had divorced myself from my feet, treating them as if they were foreign objects that were doing their best to keep me from going any further on the Camino. I yelled at them. I cursed them. I dared them to try to keep me from fulfilling my dream of walking the Camino after all these years of hoping, dreaming, and planning. I had to treat them as if they were my enemy, punishing them, torturing them for their insolence. I suppose that's how a yogi has to treat his body in order to sit motionless, meditating in the cold of winter in a mountain-top monastery: *I am not my body; it only carries me along my path. My feet are not part of me; they are my slaves to do as I wish. Their pain means nothing to me.*

This was one of the worst days. No, it was <u>the</u> worst. No question about it. I was never to experience that much pain on the Camino again.

Limping on both feet to the first bar I came to, I took a seat at an outdoor table in the shade and breathed a huge sigh of relief at having made it to Lleída where I had determined to rest an extra day in a hotel with a private bath in which to soak my feet.

As I think back I'm almost incredulous that the first entry I made in my journal that afternoon, sitting there on the street corner with heat and pain oozing from my feet, was, "The music here is as bad as in the U.S." I found popular, techno-crap music that was played in many Spanish bars and restaurants was even worse than the Top 40 stuff I'd left in the States. Unfortunately, you can't escape modern culture. And at least, if my journal is any indication, that caused me more pain than my feet.

I also noted that the country I'd walked through the last several days was mostly farmland. From one perspective it was beautiful; from another, very boring. But I noted that it gave me a lot of time for introspection: Move along, nothing to see here, just keep thinking. Which is what I had come for and mostly what I did all day.

I asked the waitress if she could refer me to a hotel that wasn't too expensive. She told me that the *Hotel Ramon Berenguer IV* was close and she thought the price was reasonable. She gave me the phone number of the hotel and I called to inquire about price and the availability of a room for one person for two nights. Forty-three Euros a night for a single was acceptable so I told the receptionist I'd be there directly. (At this point, any price would have been acceptable as long as there was a tub to soak my feet in.) I again asked the waitress if she would mind calling a cab for me. She was very kind and helpful, maybe sensing my pain and knowing that I needed help. About ten minutes later a cab stopped in the street in front of me, the driver helped me load my pack, and took me about half a kilometer to the hotel. I pretended to be embarrassed; as if I had no idea the hotel was so close! The truth was, even if I had known the hotel was only a few blocks away, I would have taken the cab.

I spent the rest of the afternoon and evening in a very nice room – modern, clean, and very comfortable. I made use of the bathtub, soaking my feet in cold water for about an hour, and then took a nice, long, hot shower, the first since I had left the states. (Forty-three Euros wasn't a lot, sure, but still, I thought it justified using somewhat more hot water than absolutely necessary.) Later that night, before bed, I soaked my feet in hot water and the following day I again performed the same cold and hot soaking procedure, which, with the day of relative rest, helped immensely.

Upon awakening the next morning I found that the hotel had a very nice breakfast, no charge for pilgrims, and I took my time enjoying all the fresh fruit, pastries, coffee (*café con leche*), and eggs I could eat, then took a cab to a bookstore where I was hoping to find a guide to the Camino in Castilian. Yes, English might have been the more practical choice: my Castilian is still far from perfect, but I wanted to challenge myself and I knew I'd be able to get by for the most part using my mid-level Spanish language skills. (Remind me to tell you later how important it is to know the word, *desvío* and the difference between *alojamientos* and *alimentos*.)

I was more than a little surprised at the cab ride to the book store.

I was raised in the American Mid-west, a child of the sixties and seventies, civil rights and all that. There is racism, prejudice, and bigotry everywhere, but it wasn't in my face in the culture in which I grew up, especially not in my home, and I don't remember it being part of my experience except one time while visiting some relatives who hadn't managed to outgrow that particular ugly side of humanity. That little experience is so memorable exactly because it was so unique in my life. At least it was until my cab ride to the book store in Lleída.

I forget how the conversation turned to the poor economic condition of Spain, but there it was, and that's all it took for the cab driver to give me his opinion on the subject, which was mainly centered around the fact that the problems in Spain were primarily the cause of the banks, and of course the banks were primarily owned by, you guessed it, *The Jews*. There was a not-so-subtle tone of, "if it weren't for The Jews we'd all be a lot better off." I wasn't in an argumentative mood, and even if I had been, my Spanish wasn't nearly good enough to carry on a reasoned discussion, as if that might even be possible with someone whose thinking is cast in a mold formed over a period of close to two thousand years, with the disastrous culmination being recent enough to be part of the memory of many still living. I was reminded of a book I had read about the history of Flamenco music and dance by a contemporary Spanish author, whose opinion, made abundantly clear in his text, was that the greatest year of Spanish history was 1492, not for the sailing of Columbus's ships, but for the expulsion of the Jews and Muslims from Spain.

As I've said before, I love Spain. But prejudice, bigotry, and ignorance are not limited to the United States.

Down, but not out. The pilgrim enjoying a cold beer and tapas in Lleída while waiting for a cab to take me to a hotel where I can rest my feet for a couple of days.

Leaving Lleída

May 27th

I don't want to offend any Catalunyans or Aragoneses who might be reading this, but I have to be honest: Looking at my journal for May 29th, I wrote, "Don't come to Catalunya or Aragon for *tapas*." (*Tapas*, plural for *tapa*, actually means "lid." In the old days, a small plate was placed on top of a glass of beer or wine to keep flies and other insects from joining in the drink. Later, restaurants began putting small appetizers on the plates. A *tapa,* then, became any type of small appetizer that is now common in almost all bars in Spain and has been raised in some establishments to a culinary art form.) I admit, I was on the Camino de Santiago. Most people on that adventure are trying to live frugally so the route doesn't attract four-star restaurants. I didn't go to any nice restaurants while on the Camino (except for one in Burgos, which will be in a future chapter), but I stopped at a lot of bars for breakfast, lunch, and dinner, and all I could write in my journal was, "The sandwiches are nothing to write home about." I didn't try all the restaurants, but over the course of a few weeks I ate at a number comprising a very respectable random sample. While I do prefer the average bar food in Catalunya and Aragon to the normal fare here in the States, I never came across a bar such as pictured here.

This is a bar in Bilbao, arrayed for breakfast, and I've been to many similar in Madrid, Seville, Granada, San Sebastian, and other Spanish cities. None along the Camino in Catalunya though. (OK, I didn't go to any bars in Barcelona. Point taken. When I return I'll make a point to sample Barcelona tapas. I'm sure they're as wonderful as the city itself.)

Getting back to the story, I spent an easy day in Lleída. I gave my feet a rest but I didn't pass up the opportunity for a little sight-seeing. After the book store, where I finally found a guide to the Camino de Santiago in Castilian, I walked a short way to the *Casco Antiguo*, the ancient part of town, and toured the cathedral and old palace grounds. There are many sources for information about the cathedral in Lleída with photos of much higher quality than I could produce, so I'm not going to spend time on that. Suffice to say that it was all very beautiful, even though the fact that the cathedral was turned into army barracks during the 18th century was a little off-putting. I was thankful, though, that the building was re-purposed rather than torn down and replaced, as it would have been in the United States. We *estado unidenses* tend to build with a sense of planned impermanence and think nothing of tearing down a two-hundred-year-old building. I looked at the beautiful stone masonry all around me and thought of Thomas Merton who said in *The Seven Story Mountain*, written between the world wars, "How does it happen that even today a couple of ordinary French stonemasons, or a carpenter and his apprentice, can put up a dovecote or a barn that has more architectural perfection than the piles of eclectic stupidity that grow up at the cost of hundreds of thousands of dollars on the campuses of American universities?" Of course, today that would be millions of dollars."

In the Cathedral of Lleída

I had an easy walk the day I left Lleída: only twenty-two kilometers. My feet were thankful. I noted in my journal that, even with a relatively short day, my energy expense was great. I wrote that even though I drank the complete three liters of water that I carried in a reservoir in my back pack, and drank as much as I could at lunch and dinner, still, I didn't urinate the entire day. (That's an easy thing for some people to say, but if you knew me, you'd know that I'm baring my soul here.) All liquids were completely perspired away. The temperatures in the afternoon hovered around 100 degrees and there was no shade anywhere on the Camino. I remembered reading about Shirley MacLaine's experiences in a book she wrote about her experiences on the Camino.

She related that one time she took an afternoon nap under a tree and had dreams of past lives in Spain. Being extremely hot and tired one day, I attempted a short siesta under a tree off the path I was walking. All I got out of it was ants; ants all over me and all over my back pack. Not a single vision of a past life to help explain what it is about Spain that makes me feel at home there. But that day, a lot of ants, if ants reincarnate, were soon dispatched to their next life.

Most days, OK, every day, I would sleep relatively late by pilgrim standards. When I got past Logroño, I found that most people arose by 6:30, many even earlier. I didn't have an alarm clock so I woke up when my body was rested. Normally I'd be on the road by 8:30 after stopping for *café con leche* and a croissant at whatever bar I passed on the way out of town. I guess I'm not a fast walker, even slower with my blistered feet, so I'd normally arrive pretty late in the day at whatever town I was to stop in for the night. I suppose this day I must have woken up early and the day's walk was relatively short, because I arrived at the pueblo where I was to stop for the night during siesta – sometime before 5:00 PM. Everything was closed. The pension where I was to spend the night, the only one in town, was closed, the bars were closed. The streets were barren. I found a small plaza with a fountain and a couple of benches under shade trees and made myself comfortable for the time being.

The view from my bench in the plaza. The water from the
fountain was ice cold and delicious.

I rested for about thirty minutes. Then, having had my fill of
cold water from the fountain, I walked around the town and
happened to find a couple of guys remodeling a house. I
asked if there might be a bar that was open during siesta
where I could wait for the pension to open and they were able
to point me to one. There I met and talked with some very
pleasant and friendly people, and had a very cold beer or two
until 5:30, at which time I went to the pension to check in.

I got there just as the owner/manager/concierge was leaving
(the place had just opened after siesta and he was leaving?),
but managed to get him to hurriedly check me in and show
me to a postage stamp-size room at the standard rate of

twenty-five Euros, dinner and wine (or water, my choice – difficult, that one) included. I showered and rested until 8:30 when dinner service began. I made my way to the dining room, and as I studied my guide, planning the next day, I enjoyed a leisurely dinner and most of the bottle of wine. Then I returned to my room for my nightly routine of blister care, and some much needed sleep.

The window faced south so there had been plenty of time for the Mediterranean sun to warm the room, and, of course, there was no air conditioning. A dog barked incessantly all night long, my feet ached, my blisters stung, and I was having the time of my life.

Parts of the Camino through Catalunya are lonely and dusty. Don't miss a yellow arrow (note the back of the sign) or you might end up in Portugal.

Lost in the Desert

May 30th

From Lleída to Zaragoza is a long, lonely stretch of the Camino. Between towns the pilgrim walks hours on end along side-roads of the N-11, the *Nacional* interstate highway. In this region, long distances of walking, commonly are broken only by the appearance of a gas station along the highway; a welcome sight where you can get a cold drink and refill your water bottles. June of 2012 was hot and dusty in that region. Spain and much of Europe was in a drought.

I had left Bujaraloz that morning sometime around 8:00. This was to be a very long day, one of the longest sections of the Camino according to my guide. I should have started out much earlier. At 8:00 AM the air was still relatively cool, but the temperature soon climbed back to the high 90s that I had become accustomed to, well over 100 degrees in the constant sun. Following my guide, I passed Hostal el Ciervo and stopped at the gas station for a cold bottle of lemonaid, then continued walking to Venta de Santa Lucia. Even doing my best to try to maintain a good walking pace, I was only walking about 5km per hour at most, so I didn't reach Venta de Santa Lucia, 20 kilometers down the road until after noon. Again, I stopped at the gas station for a cold drink and a sandwich, but didn't stay long as the route this day was 48 kilometers. Given a choice there's no way I would have walked that far in one day, but between Bujaraloz and Fuentes de Ebro there is no place to stop for the night.

Leaving Venta de Santa Lucia I was careful to follow my guide book. It said to "*leave the parking lot of the gas station and follow a path perpendicular to the Nacional, which we'll quickly leave. We'll continue through a barren and desolate territory*" Check. So far so good. Desolate and barren – good description. "*To the left, we leave the ruins of a house and continue along the path.*" House in ruins: there it is. OK, still on the right path. (I might add parenthetically that ruins of houses were common in this region of Spain, but I was pretty sure I was seeing the one to which the guide referred.) Then I watched for the sign telling me that this area was open to hunting, as described in my guidebook. Saw it. Continued on. "*... and on the right we'll see a small house on a hill.*" Yep, there it is. "*We take the camino to the right.*" My guidebook used the word "camino" which can be translated as road or path but I found later "path" is the more common usage. I thought, what road to the right? The road continues on, straight as an arrow. Did he mean this little foot path?

I'm not sure today what was meant by "camino to the right," but the only path or road I saw led into the brush, into an area from which Clint Eastwood's character would ride in one of his early spaghetti westerns. I walked along the road another half kilometer or so, watching for a road to the right. Not seeing it after some time, I backtracked and watched for any sign of the road or, even better, a rock or any sign with a yellow arrow in it directing me in the right direction, the common way of marking the Camino de Santiago. I didn't see a road or a yellow arrow, so I decided to take the path which appeared to lead nowhere, but did eventually take me to the small house on the hill. Once I reached the house, which seemed to be an old, stone, hunting cabin, abandoned and without windows or doors, I looked around, now with a better view afforded by the elevation. I couldn't see anything described in the guide.

"OK, smart guy, what are you going to do now?" I thought. I had about half of my water remaining in the 3-liter bladder in my back pack, and only a banana to eat. I didn't think going back to the dirt road and continuing on was a good idea: I could tell from the rudimentary map of the day's plan in the guide book that it led away from where I wanted to go. Looking out in the distance, there was nothing but barren desert as far as I could see. Looking at the map in the guide book, I could tell which direction I eventually needed to go to reach Fuentes de Ebro, and even though I had no watch I knew it was well after noon, so the sun was in the southwest. If I headed northwest I would eventually run into the *Nacional* and I could follow that to Fuentes de Ebro. It was a simple plan and it worked. Keeping my shadow ahead of me and to my right, I began walking cross country through the desert of Aragón. I was confident that I'd reach the highway, but between here and there I didn't know what I'd run into. I knew I was in a perfect area for snakes so I kept a wary eye for them. I saw a few, but they saw me first and I'd only catch a glimpse of their tails as they'd slither away.

After about an hour and a half I reached the *Nacional* and began walking along it in the direction of my destination. According to the small map in my guide book, the Camino was supposed to get close to the *Nacional* and I hoped I hadn't passed that point, wanting to get away from the highway and into quieter, safer conditions. The highway was a constant stream of trucks with no place to walk other than between the guard rail and the road. Trucks zoomed within feet of me at a frightful speed, bumper to bumper, more like a train than individual vehicles. I'd never seen a highway so packed with traffic moving so fast. I wasn't afraid of being hit by a truck, but I'd seen a truck tire come apart – tread separation – large sections flying along the highway at 60 miles an hour. A human didn't stand a chance against that.

Well, here I am writing, so obviously no truck tire section hit me and I came through the experience unscathed. I'm sure a lot of truckers were thinking, "*loca folla!*"(Crazy fucker! (It doesn't sound that bad in Spanish.)) I finally found the Camino and happily left the highway.

The view from the little house on the hill. No Camino in sight,
but the highway is out there somewhere.

I didn't know if my detour resulted in a shortening or lengthening of that day's plan, but I know I put in somewhere close to 48 kilometers; the longest day of the Camino, and most exhausting, even without the little trek through the desert.

But I got through it – through the heat, through the desert, snakes, tumbleweeds, and worst of all, within an arm's length of a few thousand trucks passing me at 100 Km per hour. I ran out of water well before I reached Fuentes de Ebro and was fairly starving when I finally got the chance to eat. But I made it. I thanked God, my guardian angels, Saint James,

Jesus, and anyone else who might have been listening to a weary pilgrim.

Zaragoza

June 1st

Here's where the story gets a little sketchy for quite a while. I had purchased a guide to the Camino through Catalunya and Aragon at the book store in Lleída and, being somewhat lazy (if you can call a person who walks over 850 miles across Spain lazy) I made most of my notes in the guide book rather than my journal. It seemed like the right thing to do at the time. The guide had all the cities and route markings, with notes about hostels and albergues and interesting things to see along the way. I made my own notes of my thoughts and things that happened in the guide alongside the route information in that book.

Sadly, the notes I took in my guide are now lost. As every pilgrim knows, any time you can save weight in your pack, you do so. I had already given away the tent that apparently I was not going to need. Then, sometime after Logroño, in the region of La Rioja, Castilla-Leon, I found a post office and purchased a small *"caja verde,"* a green box that comes in three sizes that the Spanish post office sells for easy shipment of small goods. I shipped the guide containing my notes along with a pair of light walking shoes that no longer fit due to the swelling of my feet, a small book of stunning Camino photographs by a photographer who had an exhibit of her work in an ancient church in a town in which I had stopped, and a few other things I found I did not need. I did not purchase insurance, as the things I sent were not that valuable, at least, not monetarily. Sadly, neither did I ship my goods using a traceable method. When I returned to the States I found that the box had been opened and the Camino guide and book of photographs had been stolen. I contacted the Spanish Customs office to inquire whether someone might have opened the box for inspection and neglected to replace everything that was in it, hoping that I might be able to start a trace of my goods that might result in their being found. The customs office wrote back to tell me that they did not open mail leaving the country, and that they had contacted the Spanish mail service about the matter. The Spanish mail service, of course, had no information about my books. Case closed. The same thing happened with another box I sent later from Granada, before returning to the States and, of course, before finding that the first box had been tampered with. The second box, however, was completely emptied. Several books in Hebrew were put in it, I suppose for weight, and most likely taken from another customer's shipment, and sent on to me. Again, the contents weren't insured. In that box I had put several pieces of gear I'd need for my next pilgrimage along with a high-quality (read: expensive) Barcelona *futbol* jersey which I'd bought for my son. The gear I have since replaced, and will buy another jersey for my son when I return to Spain. But in that box I had also placed my

Compostela, the certificate you get in Santiago after completing the Camino, and more importantly, my pilgrim credentials – that record with unique stamps of every city and pueblo that I had passed through from Montserrat to Finisterre. I have since been able to get a copy of my *Compostela* from the Pilgrim Office in Santiago, but the pilgrim credentials are lost forever. I try, am trying, to be stoic about the loss of my pilgrim credential. It's only a thing. I would have framed it and placed it on a wall to gather dust. It wouldn't have affected my life to have it, to be able to look at it. But I'm human, and the credential was a representation of the completion of a long-held dream and a physically and emotionally demanding experience with a dated, unique stamp of every pueblo and city I passed through. And unlike my sleeping bag, inflatable mattress, boots (good riddance), and other outdoor gear, it does whoever has it absolutely no good. Truth is, it was probably thrown in a trash can. I suppose it's a good exercise in letting go.

So here I am. The next entry in my journal is from Zaragoza, where I again stayed an extra day to allow my feet some R&R. As I remember my entry into this beautiful city, I seemed to have walked forever and was concerned that I had missed a turn that would take me into the city. Some kilometers from the borders of the city the Camino intersects, and becomes, a nature trail on its outskirts. Doing my best to read my Castilian (Spanish) guide, I was fairly certain I was on the right path, but things just didn't seem right. As the path was frequented by runners and cyclists I had a few opportunities to ask if I might have missed a turn and was passing Zaragoza. I was assured that I was still on the right track, but as I got closer to the city the guide seemed to be less and less helpful. I finally ignored it and followed trail signs into the city. I remember making a note in my guide that it was fairly useless on the entry to this particular city.

Once I got to the outskirts of Zaragoza I thought I might never find the center of the city where the guide said there was a hostel and of course, *La Basílica de Nuestra Señora del Pilar*. It seemed that I had already walked ten kilometers from the outskirts of the city and still no *Plaza del Pilar* and the great basilica. But I kept walking; faith and a sense of direction leading me on. I asked directions once or twice, finding I was on the right street; I just had to keep walking. I finally reached the plaza, where, true to form, I sat down at the nearest bar and had a cold beer and tapas, admiring the cathedral (*La Catedral de la Seo*, which was converted and built up from an even older mosque, right next to the basilica), the basilica itself, the fountains, the sculpture, and the pure beauty that surrounded me, thanking God and my guardian angels that I had made it this far in good health (albeit with a few blisters – a minor inconvenience).

The next order of business was to find a hostel where I could store my pack so I could wander the plaza area and enjoy myself without being concerned with all my worldly belongings. I found one nearby where I experienced my first communal sleeping arrangement of the Camino. Never underestimate the importance of a good set of earplugs. Like good socks and hiking boots, good earplugs are an item without which one cannot even think of attempting the Camino.

My only regret is that, with all the sights in Zaragoza, I spent the next day resting and never ventured far from the plaza, the shops, and bars nearby to view the other interesting sites in that city. But I had my feet and my budget to think of, and for one day, I thoroughly enjoyed myself wandering around an area not greater than about four city blocks.

Pausing at mid-day for lunch and a bottle of wine I observed a wedding party entering the basilica. Being completely honest, I have to say that the bottle of wine somewhat greased the skids and I decided to wander across the square and take a look. The wedding Mass was just starting and it just seemed like the right thing to do to take a seat at the back of the basilica and take part in the Mass. After all, it was a regularly scheduled Mass, there just happened to be a wedding ceremony included for no extra charge. I hadn't attended Mass for a couple of years at least; vespers at the Cathedral of Montserrat didn't count. As usual, I understood very little of what was being said, but I was familiar with the ordinary of the Mass and I knew what was going on except for the wedding parts.

I don't understand exactly why or how, but I got completely absorbed in the ceremony. Chalk it up to the Camino, the time I had over the last couple of weeks for introspection, listening, experiencing, being in the moment, the painful feet, the exhilaration of the whole Spanish experience, the complete change of environment. And I don't discount the wine – one of God's gifts to mankind. It was completely unplanned but I went forward for communion and followed the line back to my pew, kneeled, and said prayers for myself and everyone I could think of. At the end of the Mass I joined the line of people entering a tiny chapel where we kissed the feet of a statue of Jesus and knelt in front of a small, ornate, gold-trimmed alter for more prayer. Tears began to flow from my eyes, by body was wracked by tension and release. I had no idea what was happening to me or why, I didn't have a clear thought in my head. All I knew was that something was being released at that moment that I needed to shed at Jesus' feet and I allowed it to flow. I don't normally follow the rituals of the Church – kneeling, bowing, Stations of the Cross, communion – but this day it seemed right to do so and I followed the lead of whatever spirits were urging me and felt completely right about doing so.

Following this, after taking some time to allow my eyes to dry, I went back to the plaza and walked up and down, looking at whatever was in front of my eyes, trying to memorize everything as if I'd never be able to see again, to absorb not only the look of the architecture, statues, and fountains, but to smell any scents I could pick up, to hear all the sounds, and feel the stone work of the walls of the Basilica. I knew I might never experience this again and I didn't want to waste the opportunity to be completely absorbed in this magical place.

A Wedding Mass in *La Basílica de Nuestra Señora del Pilar*

Later, I toured the *Catedral de la Seo* which began its life as
a mosque (beautiful, gorgeous, stunning, awe-inspiring: all
words are inadequate to describe this mosque cum cathedral)
and had lunch in an Irish bar where I had a very nice

conversation in English with the bartender. It was the perfect way to decompress from the emotional roller coaster of the last few hours.

All in all, the two days I spent in Zaragoza comprise some of my best memories of the Camino to that point.

Someday I'll return.

The cathedral roof line (a small part of it, anyway)

Torres de Barrellén

June 3rd

Another day of rest was what my feet needed. They were still blistered and sore when I left Zaragoza, but as I review my journal I see that the worst seems to be over. I left Zaragoza with the best of pilgrim intentions, planning to walk every step of the way. But leaving the hostel, I followed my guide to the letter; of that, I'm sure. I walked up and down streets, following my guide, seeing what it told me I should see, turning where it said to turn, only to lose the signs and end up where I was certain I was not supposed to be. I watched for the yellow arrows that would direct me back to the Camino but after three or four unfruitful attempts to get back on the path I accepted defeat and hailed a cab. Zaragoza is a large city, one of the largest that one passes through on the Camino Catalan from Montserrat. I hope I'll be forgiven for cheating just a little and taking a cab to the outskirts of town to the sports complex where I easily found that little yellow arrow painted on the street, directing me toward Santiago de Compostela.

My journal tells me that I was looking forward to a change of scenery; the constant view of nothing but flat farmland makes for long days. The constant heat, somewhere around 100 degrees every day, walking in the sun, added to the exhaustion factor at the end of each day. And, while the albergues in Catalunya and Aragon were mostly free (I had to pay five or seven euros at only two of them) for the most part I was staying in hostels at a normal rate of 25 Euros a night, about 34 dollars at today's exchange rate. I was also spending more on food than I had planned. I hadn't found any of those cheap "pilgrim specials" that I had read about. A normal breakfast was coffee and a croissant for about two Euros. A second coffee was another euro – no free refills in Spain. Lunch would be a sandwich and a beer for six or seven, dinner was normally the *menú del día* – salad and some kind of pasta with chicken or a filet (cheap cut of steak) for around ten or eleven Euros. It wasn't unusual to spend 40 to 45 Euros a day, or about 55 dollars. What kept me from being too worried about the money was that I knew that once I reached Logroño, my lodging expenses would decrease and I'd read that albergues normally had kitchens, so I wouldn't have to eat three meals a day in restaurants.

June 3rd, Torres de Barrellén and an albuergue for only six Euros. Wa-hoo!! My guide suggested continuing on to Alagón, but there was no albergue there and, as usual, my feet were dying. Better to save the money, give my feet an easy day and stop here. Finally, as I noted in my journal, this day I found no new blisters: A first! The temperatures had also moderated so I was a happy pilgrim. Here in Torres de Barrellén I again had the albergue all to myself so I had a peaceful night's sleep. I say this with the memory of almost every night that I spent in an albergue after Logroño where I had to share a room, being one of snoring, only mitigated, barely, by my ear plugs.

The beautiful architecture of the Muslim and Mudehar heritage of Spain

I was walking the Camino hoping to have some spiritual renewal, awakening, rebirth – something! – to find that "still small voice" of God to which I had seemed to be deaf my entire life. So far, I had heard nothing but the constant tape loop in my brain that played the list of my shortcomings, of my financial stupidity, the memories of failed relationships and people I'd hurt and disappointed along the way, interspersed with my musings on the abysmal state of politics and economics in the United States.

But I was patient. It was early and I still had most of the Camino ahead of me. At the same time, I was thoroughly enjoying the environment – just being in Spain with no telephone, no computer, no television, no one depending on me to be anywhere, no one asking for status reports or to schedule or attend meetings, no need to make any decisions other than when to get out of bed and start walking every day. While each day was tiring, each day was tiring in a good way; from the ankles up I was healthy and fully capable of whatever physical stresses the Camino put before me, and even my feet now seemed to be on the mend. I read in one of the books about the Camino de Santiago before undertaking the journey that everyone finds some point on the Camino where they ask themselves, "What am I doing here?" and wondering if it might not be a good idea to stop, take a bus to the nearest airport, and fly back home. I can honestly and sincerely say that I never got to that point. From the day I arrived in Barcelona to the "End of the Earth," Finisterre, I was in a state of contentment such as I had never known, and, as I said in an earlier chapter, one that I fear I will never find again.

A windy day walking through the *llanura* of Aragon

Polígonos

(Here comes an aside, a political rant. Skip to the next chapter if you want; It won't hurt my feelings, much.)

Walking across Catalunya and Aragon, as I entered several larger towns and cities, through the outskirts of the town I would occasionally walk past *polígonos* – industrial parks – brand new, huge buildings, gated, secure properties with sprawling parking lots, brand new lighted streets leading up to and surrounding them, the concrete still gleaming white, new and unmarked by graffiti—

Sitting lonely and vacant.

These are Spain's ghost *polígonos*, some complete with tumbleweeds, evidence of low interest rates and easy money provided courtesy of European politicians and central banks. I was a ground-level witness to the inexplicable wastefulness of Keynesian economics in action. Or rather, inaction. Where did the money come from to build these acres upon acres of factory and office buildings? Was it stolen from the people of Spain and the rest of the Euro-zone in the form of taxes? Or was it just created out of thin air, a tax on future generations who would have to suffer the devalued currency that would necessarily result from the creation of hundreds of billions of Euros that provided nothing more and nothing less than some politician's wet dream of a new industrial park in his district?

75

Whence came the demand for these industrial parks? Whom was the potential productive capacity of the factories and offices going to help? What additional productive, economic activity would cover the costs of the land, building materials, and construction costs of these grand albatrosses hung around the collective necks of the people of Spain? And where was the evidence that the billions of Euros spent on these *polígonos* was the best use of the capital, even if it was counterfeit, created out of nothing?

"If you build it, they will come" only works in movies. In the real world, where people risk their real saving, saving which represents real and valuable productivity over and above what its creator had expended in the past, an investment in a *polígono* or a store front or a restaurant or any business enterprise would be undertaken after a careful business and economic analysis gave evidence of an imbalance between supply and demand which the new business enterprise would then be able exploit (in an economic sense), hopefully at a profit. But as there was no demand for these industrial parks, after they were built they sat empty, a monument to wastefulness and the hubris of pseudo-intellectual politicians and economicians who thought they could affect and change human nature and the laws of economics.

In the world of politics and Keynesian economics, money is created out of nothing and spread around in direct correlation with the power of the politicians who wield it. The money the politician is spending is not his, it is not the fruit of his labors, he hasn't reduced his past consumption in order to save for a future investment in an enterprise that will improve the general welfare and produce future profits.

No, the source of his money is always the productive capacity of those who have earned it, and then is stolen via taxes, or it is stolen from those in the future who will have to earn it by the sweat of their face to pay the required taxes to pay off the bonds or to produce more for a greater amount of the inflated currency which buys less and less.

But this is of no consequence to the politician who is the beneficiary of the newly created Euros (or dollars or pesos or yen or…). He and his cronies are the first beneficiaries of his inflated government salary and whatever he can skim off the top for himself. The hundreds of billions changing hands in government offices, before the money enters circulation and becomes worth-less, are manna from heaven for the politically well-connected. The politician doesn't have to produce, save, or plan for the future, except in so far as he plans how much he can extort from the political system to support his extravagant lifestyle at the expense of the people he is supposed to represent. He and his family will be fine. It is the rest, the mundanes, the non-politically connected peons who have to suffer from the inflated currency and ill-spent money on unneeded and unwanted *polígonos*, standing empty, rusting, collecting dust, doing nothing more than providing gleaming white horizontal surfaces for yet more graffiti.

Luceni

June 4th

Well, there you have it: my thoughts on the economic condition of the world in the microcosm of Spanish industrial parks. Much as I wanted to leave all worldly concerns behind and concentrate on my internal struggles and find a new path (a new camino – the symbolism did not escape me), the cancer on the Earth that is the political class hovered over my head constantly and consistently as I walked, albeit further away than in the past, at times so far away that I didn't notice it. Sometimes several hours would pass without the oppressive, frustrating thoughts of the political class and how they ruin life for the rest of us. To this I owe the lack of television and newspapers. Whenever I'd stop in a bar for breakfast, lunch, or dinner I'd consciously avoid the television if it was tuned to a news program. Thankfully, the normal fare was *futbol* (soccer here in the U.S.) I consciously avoid television. I'm sure there is something worth spending an hour to watch on occasion, but I always think of the story of the boy who, presented a room piled to the ceiling with horse manure, became very excited and began digging through the manure, saying, "I'm sure there's a horse in here somewhere." Call me a pessimist, but if there's a thoroughbred horse in all the manure that is today's television fare, he'll just have to stay buried. As for me, I'd rather walk anyway.

We'll get back to the Camino, but first...

Before I left the States I started weaning myself off of my twenty-year reliance on anti-depressants, my vitamin P as it is referred to by some. I'd let a day go by without taking it during the week, then a couple of days, taking it four or five days a week, then down to skipping a day out of every three. I noticed no difference in my mood, although a "professional" would probably say, "Of course you noticed no difference – you're too close to the subject." Self-un-medication, as with self-medication, is a dangerous path which should be left to the professionals.

I'm not so sure. I like to live dangerously. Sometimes I don't floss my teeth. I jay-walk. I don't have a 401K. I use salad dressing that is past its expiration date. Through the pain of my bad feet, the heat of Catalunya and Aragon, and the solitude of those first weeks on the Camino, even without my Prozac, I felt good. No, not just good, I felt great, ecstatic, energetic every day. I ate well. I slept well, I enjoyed life. I enjoyed the sound of the rushing water through the irrigation canals along the Camino and the view of the Rio Ebro as I walked along it day after day. In the heat of Aragon, when I'd come across irrigation sprinklers overshooting the field I'd stand in the spray of water to cool off and simply enjoy the feel of the water on my head and face, soaking my shirt. I had no idea what each day would bring and I wasn't yet at the point where I thought about life after I'd reached Santiago (that was where I could have used some Prozac, I'll admit). All I knew was that every day was good. Damn good, in fact.

Before entering Luceni, as I walked along the Rio Ebro, I came upon a small town that featured a bronze statue of Sancho Panza, Don Quixote's faithful squire. I had first read that book in high school, then again several years ago. It is, without a doubt, my favorite book in the whole world, not only because of the masterful writing, but because I identify so strongly with the The Don. Book One of Don Quixote is written as a parody of popular chivalric literature of the time. The Don and his faithful squire are simpletons and the butt of jokes. But the theme of the second book, written ten years after the first, gives us an entirely different perspective on Don Quixote and Sancho, using the pair as a representation of the "wisdom of foolishness," and showing the "foolishness of the wise" ruling classes. In a couple of chapters of the second book of that first and greatest of all modern novels, Sancho is given Barataria Island to govern by a pair of dukes as a practical joke on poor Sancho (Barataria is from barata, which means "cheap, of low or no value" in Spanish). The dukes, representing the political class of the day, try to snare Sancho in intrigue and political problems of the island. Sancho, however, applies common sense and practical, down-to-earth wisdom to evade and avoid the snares and shows the foolishness of the learned dukes. Throughout the second book Sancho and Don Quixote take on entirely different characters from the first. This is where we find the spirit of what was to become the famous musical, "*Man of La Mancha*:" dreaming the impossible dream, reaching beyond hope. It matters not whether there is any possibility of success, for the success is in the attempt itself, born of the dream.

Sancho Panza and I, resting near the Rio Ebro and Isla Barataria.

In Luceni, my guide said there was a beautiful, 13th century church. I didn't find it, but I didn't really look very hard. My only concern was food, cold beer, and a good night's sleep. I noted in my journal that "The weather continued to be pleasant, if a little windy, but nothing like the first two days out of Montserrat. Still no word from God."

I felt fortunate that Luceni had an albergue, even though it was nothing more than a mattress on the floor of a large multi-purpose room in the building that housed the *ayuntamiento*. On the Camino, one is grateful for small favors, even a hard floor in a gym.

It seemed to be the norm in most small Spanish pueblos that the streets were deserted in the afternoon. I wandered into town not having any idea where the *ayuntamiento* was. Normally you'd find it at one of the main plazas, or The *Plaza Mayor* if the town had one. Luceni didn't seem to have a plaza, much less a *Plaza Mayor*. The town seemed to be a relatively modern creation; not like most of the other pueblos I'd walk through on the Camino, obviously several hundred years old. I attempted to ask a woman on the street if she could direct me, but was ignored as she hurried on her way, the first and only time help wasn't offered willingly and gladly during my entire four months in Spain. I found a main street and what looked like the town's largest *bar restaurante* and, after the requisite beer, asked where I might find the *ayuntamiento* and was directed to an address where someone would have the key, as the *ayuntamiento* was not open. What seemed very odd at the time, but became the norm in so many towns through Catalunya and Aragon, was that I was given the key to a municipal building as if I were a long-time, trusted resident of the town rather than a passing vagabond. The Camino is like that: everyone trusts pilgrims (except the one woman noted above) and pilgrims trust everyone. (I was reminded of a scene in *Under the Tuscan Sun* in which the main character is buying an Italian villa. Before the paperwork is complete she is given the keys to the house and told she can move in. She seems incredulous. She could have the house before all the paperwork was complete? The woman handling the transaction said, "It's a house, not a moped. What are you going to do? Steal it?" I guess that's what the people at the *ayuntamiento* thought and is completely reasonable. But still, an American, used to the security state that this country has become, is taken aback by such behavior.) Through 1,250 kilometers and fifty days on the Camino, I didn't hear a word of anyone experiencing any dangerous situations, theft, or violence. I imagine that a protective energy field pervades the Camino on all the routes from all the source cities, built up from what I can only call a "spiritual residue" from over a thousand years and millions of pilgrims making their way to Santiago that no negative energy can invade.

Getting back to Luceni, a very friendly and helpful woman, the norm on the Camino, showed me to the albergue, gave me my choice of mattresses, being the only pilgrim at the albergue yet again, handed me the key, asked me to leave it at her door in the morning if she wasn't available, and wished me a pleasant night. There was neither shower nor hot water, but there was a soft mattress and after a simple dinner at the bar I spent another night in blissful sleep.

I awoke the next morning at about 8:00 and went back to the bar for my breakfast of *café con leche* and a croissant, spending about an hour talking with a woman who was interested in my Camino experience, finally hitting the road at about 9:30, again, very late by pilgrim standards. But what did I know? I was still traveling solo and every day was an adventure into the unknown.

Tudela

June 5th

I reached Ribaforera after walking 34 kilometers that day to find there was no albergue, no pension, nor hostel in the town.

I know what you're thinking; "Didn't your guide tell you that there was no place to stay in Ribaforera?" Yes, it did, and it took me several more weeks to realize the difference between *alojamientos* and *alimentos*. A Spanish speaker would realize that those are two completely separate, distinct words, not sounding at all alike. But a novice in the language (yours truly, for instance), I hope can be forgiven for confusing the two. The first means lodging, the second, food. I read in my guide book that Ribaforera had no *alojamientos* and I thought, how strange not to have any food in town. I thought that must mean there was no grocery store; that this pueblo must be so small that the residents have to drive to a larger town to go shopping for food. It never occurred to me that my guide was telling me that there was no place to spend the night, that there was no hotel, hostel, albergue, nothing. Imagine my consternation when I found out what *alojamientos* meant. As Homer Simpson put it, "Marge, sometimes I'm just not very bright."

I had given away my tent in Lleída, but there was no place to camp anyway. Walking another kilometer, much less another

12 to the next town was not an option. The rule (actually more of a guideline) of the pilgrimage to Santiago de Compostela is that you don't take the bus or a cab unless you're not physically able to proceed on your chosen means of locomotion – walking or bicycling, normally, although there are those who make the Camino on horseback. Well, I was not able to proceed on my miserable feet even one more kilometer, so it was time to admit defeat for the day, hop on a bus, and get to the next town where I could check into a nice pension or hostel and get some rest. Reluctantly, I boarded a bus for Tudela.

A church tower in Tudela

Arriving at the central bus station, I had no idea where I was. The guide had me entering on foot in some other part of town and this was no small pueblo where I could just wander around until I found the *Plaza Mayor* and the *Ayuntamiento*.

Tudela was a genuine *ciudad*, a city, and relative to most other towns I had passed through or would pass through on the remainder of the Camino, a big city at that. I've already broken the rules and ridden a bus, so what's one more transgression? I'll take a taxi to the *Casco Antiguo* where my pilgrim guide says I can find a pension. (No albergue here.) Problem was, I waited at the taxi stand for about thirty minutes without a taxi in sight. Better said, there was one taxi in sight but its driver had made himself scarce. Maybe it was break time. Or he just had better things to do. At any rate, I started wandering toward where my intuition told me I'd find the center of town, until I happened upon a young couple of whom I asked directions. They told me I was heading in the right direction: just go up the hill, turn right, continue up the hill, turn left, then up another hill, another right at the *farmácia*…

It sounded like another five-K and all uphill. I asked them if I might just take a cab and they told me that cars are not allowed in the *Casco Antiguo*.

I'd have to walk. But realizing the directions were too complicated, or a better guess, that my Spanish was not up to the task of adequately understanding what they were saying, they invited me to walk with them and they would show me the way. By this time I was used to people being bend-over-backwards friendly and helpful so I went along for the ride. We had a pleasant conversation, most of which I don't remember, but part of it was about the difficulty of learning a foreign language. They wanted to learn English and I thought, "Wonderful! My first two students! If only I were planning to remain in Tudela." Of course, I wasn't, but I was encouraged nevertheless. As I spoke with people and they would ask me where I was from, I'd tell them I last lived in the U.S., but currently had no address and was, in effect, homeless, but I hoped to stay in Spain and teach English for a living. I received encouragement from everyone. Even when talking about the problems of working illegally before I could establish residence, everyone, to a person, told me not to worry about it. Just plop myself down somewhere, find some private students, and in three years I could apply for residency. Sounded easy. Maybe this was why I was so happy on the Camino: The future I had dreamed of seemed to be finally within reach.

They walked with me to the old part of town and led me to the street where my guidebook said I'd find a pension. I expressed my thanks for going out of their way to bring me here, and we said our farewells. It turned out to be only about a ten- or twelve-minute walk. Coming to a, you guessed it, bar, I sat down and ordered a very cold beer. Ah, the small pleasures of the Camino!

A sign on an ancient building across the street told me that it was a pension but as was typical much of the time, there was no open front entrance, lobby, check-in desk, or any visible way to gain access to a room. I asked the bartender at the bar if he knew how I could get a room there and he told me to wait, and that he'd get the manager. In a few minutes a short, surly, man greeted me. I introduced myself as a pilgrim and asked if there were a room available for one night in the pension. He told me there was, gave me the price, which I think was 22 Euros, said he'd get a key and show me to a room and then was gone. No "I'll be right back," or "Hang on a second," or "Please enjoy your beer while I get the key." He just walked away.

This was my introduction to what I would find was a grand tradition in Granada, but which I also found throughout Spain – the *mala folla*, or, not to be too delicate about the translation, *the surly fucker*. This is an attitude not dissimilar to what you might find in Northern New Jersey or the South side of Chicago. It's the "I know who I am but who the hell are you" attitude. In fact, the normal greeting I received when entering a bar in Granada was, directly translated, "Talk to me." Sometimes it was, loosely translated,"waddya want?" And in fact, if I said something to the effect of, "I would like a beer, please," the look I'd get was one that said, "You *would* like a beer if… what?" As if an attitude of politeness was not only unwelcome, but I was wasting their time by using unnecessary syllables and the present subjunctive tense. The Irish bartender in Zaragoza told me that this was one thing he still hadn't gotten used to after living and working in Spain for ten years. The typical phrasing used to request a beer in a bar is, loosely translated, "Gimme a beer." In fact, the bartender told me that one time he and his fellow bartenders had started ringing a bell any time a customer used the word "please" or left a tip. Sometime around midnight, at hearing the bell, the bartender's boss asked him why he rang the bell. The bartender explained, and the manager said, incredulously, "And you've only rung it twice all night?"

Getting back to the story, the manager returned after I had had time to drink a second beer (Could that have been his plan the whole time?), showed me to my room, gave me the key and said I could pay him later. He hadn't taken my name, hadn't asked for ID, hadn't asked for payment, yet still gave me the key and left me alone. Absolute trust, no checking of ID for alcohol purchases, and friendly people (other than bartenders). This country was going to take some getting used to.

I showered, cared for my feet – although there were no new blisters, I was still caring for the old ones nightly – and returned to the bar for a dinner of chicken penne in a red sauce, salad, and a couple of glasses of wine. OK, maybe more than a couple. As I think I've said, normally with dinner you get your choice of a bottle of water or a bottle of wine. Take your pick. And I'll say once more, tough choice, that one.

Sometime between dinner and going to bed the manager knocked on my door to ask for the 22 Euros, with a look that said, "Hey buddy, howz about the money you owe?" *Mala folla*. I told him I had looked for him at the restaurant but hadn't seen him. He seemed satisfied, took the cash, and left.

The night was hot and my window overlooked a street containing several bars. I'd been to Spain before and knew what to expect – this is a noisy country. I closed the window, inserted my ear plugs, and slept the sleep of the dead the whole night.

Alfaro and Arrúbal

June 6th

D-Day. St. Norbert's Day. My sister's birthday. The day I got to Alfaro in Aragon, the wine country of La Rioja, home of the largest population of storks in the world.

In the summer, on the roof of Colegiata San Miguel, you'll find over 500 (yes, five <u>hundred!</u>) storks. The clicking sound they make with their beaks is as constant as the rising of the sun. In other cities and towns I heard the incessant screeching of swallows as they darted through the air, keeping the bug population to a comfortable level. But in Alfaro, storks rule the skies and the top of every tower or high place they can find. I saw storks all through Aragon and into Castilla y Leon. Their nests seemed to be on every tall structure available – power line towers, church towers, office buildings, anything over a hundred feet tall seemed to have a giant stork's nest on top of it. The size of the sticks they use to build their nests – some appeared to be veritable branches – attests to the strength of these birds. It's no wonder they're used to deliver babies.

Storks are everywhere

The blisters on my feet were finally healing and turning into calluses, but I was beginning to have problems with the fact that there wasn't enough room in the toe box of my boots for my toes. I believe it was somewhere near Alfaro that I cut a hole in the side of my right boot to give the little toe of that foot some room. It was probably another hundred kilometers down the road when I cut another hole for my big toe. I didn't have to "customize" my left boot – the left foot is slightly smaller than the right and I managed to get by, although I did lose two toenails on that foot by the end of the Camino. I believe I paid about $200 for those boots but I couldn't see any good reason to not make whatever "modifications" might help me survive the next several hundred kilometers.

It was also at this point that my camera battery decided to give up the ghost. The camera uses a battery specific to the camera, not a standard double- or triple-A, so my only option was to recharge it. I can be very absent-minded; ask any woman with whom I've had a relationship. It seems to be something that drives them nuts. I don't care much for the characteristic myself, but I've learned to live with it. Not so with my various women friends. Anyway, back to the story. I had brought my recharger, but thought I'd be able to purchase a power converter easily along the way. The power converter I already owned was a large and heavy kit that included a plug for every country in the world: way too impractical for the Camino. Yes, I could have taken just the converter plug for Spain, but for some reason two different plug types in the kit were labeled for Europe and I didn't want to carry anything unnecessary, especially since I thought it would be easy to find just what I needed in Spain. My mistake was in thinking I could buy anything easily along the way. The towns I passed through seemed to be too small for a shop that carried many of the things I needed – a hat, a guide to the Camino, a power converter – or I'd pass through during siesta when everything was closed. The power converter proved to be exceptionally difficult to find, so I spent the next several days sans camera.

Thinking back, my idea of finding a power converter along the way was pretty silly. Why would a shop in any small town in Spain stock a power converter for U.S. to Spanish plugs? As it turned out, I found out later that the charger for my Canon camera accepted both 120- and 240-volt sources, so all I needed was a plug converter which was available in any general store. Live and learn.

Another couple of days passed before I made another entry in my journal. June 8th. I spent the night in Arrúbal, in the *Ayuntamiento*, on the floor, at no charge. Again, I was grateful for small favors.

With a dead camera battery I can't even look back at pictures to try to remember where I was. I hope that if anything interesting happened I would have written about it in my journal, but for the most part my pilgrimage to this point was one of self-discovery, contemplation, observation, listening to the silence as I'd walk through the Spanish countryside, and most of all, simply enjoying the days passing without a phone call, without being concerned with email, without a television and its incessant blathering news, without seeing the face or name of Obama or any other American politician. That alone would have made the pilgrimage worth all the foot pain and dehydration and getting lost in the Aragon desert.

The next day I would enter Logroño, where my route would join that of the more common and popular French route from Saint Jean Pied de Port. This is where the Camino would more closely resemble the books I'd read and the movie, *The Way*, which I highly recommend, even though it is impossible to capture the true, life changing nature of the Camino in a two-hour movie. I have to say though, after watching it three times, prior to my own Camino experience, the director and actors did a good job of getting close to the mood of the Camino and giving a sense of the camaraderie, self-discovery, and growth that one might experience. Today, after the Camino, I can't watch the movie because it brings back so many memories; memories I cannot bear at the moment without suffering a near emotional breakdown. More than a year after I completed the Camino I'm still suffering from a mild PTSD, Post-Traumatic Stress Syndrome, except in my case the trauma was caused by an experience so wonderful that I find it difficult to proceed with a normal life. Even writing about it now, after more than a year has elapsed, can be incredibly difficult.

I remember feeling that I was going to be starting a new Camino in Logroño. When I started in Montserrat I had no idea what to expect, I was walking into an unknown world. After 20 days I had developed a routine, but it was my routine – all me, all day. I got up when I wanted, stopped when I wanted, walked at my pace (slowly, it turns out). I wondered if after Logroño I'd become part of a group (yes, I did), If I'd be able to sleep in a communal bunk-house with people snoring (yes, with earplugs), if I'd miss my private time. This one isn't a parenthetical thought. No, I didn't miss my private time because I found the people on the Camino were the warmest, most interesting, most engaging people I'd ever met. Oh, there was a bore here and there but they were very few and far between and you didn't have to hang around with anyone you didn't care to be with. I'm sure that has something to do with a combination of the type of person who is willing to go on a walk of 500, 800, 1,000 miles, some even more, and the attitude a pilgrim develops as the days and miles pass by on the Camino. You don't know what to expect at any time and you develop an attitude of gratitude for every small favor. All along the way you receive favors and you give favors; you help where help is needed and gratefully accept any level of assistance you receive from other pilgrims, the townspeople you meet along the way, and the saints who run the albergues.

At the time I felt that my time for reflection and spiritual renewal was coming to an end, and I'd now just join a large group of people walking by day and partying by night. I thought I'd miss my solitary Camino experience. I couldn't have been more wrong.

Of Olives and Prozac

It seems a good time to make a few notes of things I've thought of that don't fit very well into my daily narrative. So, if you will, permit me a little break for some random thoughts.

Olives:

Why is it so difficult in the United States to find olives with pits in them? One of my favorite things about stopping at a bar for a beer or a glass of wine was that I could always get a plate of olives and bread with olive oil to dip it in. (I can't help mention once more that I was never carded when ordering a beer or wine. Is Spain a great country or what?) I'd enjoy the cold beer in the hundred-degree heat, or later in Galicia where it was cooler, a glass of wine, while slowly eating the olives, working around the pit with my teeth and tongue, getting the meat of the olive on one side of my mouth, holding the pit in the cheek of the other side, then chewing the remaining meat of the olive off the pit after swallowing the easy part. I didn't do as good a job as a friend I met on the Camino, who would get every last bit of meat off the pit, and then even bite the pit in half to get at the little olive tree inside it. I aspired to her talent but knew that it would take years to attain, so I just sat in admiration. Now that I'm back in the States, I haven't been able to find a jar of olives with the pits still in them. They're always stuffed with something – blue cheese, anchovies, garlic, pimientos – anything but the pit that God made them with. *¿Porque?* I'm a staunch, free-market capitalist so I understand supply and demand and the fact that those who sell olives want to supply what the market wants to buy. So the question is, why do so few Americans know of the pleasure of eating olives with the pits still in them? Is it cultural? Do we in the U.S. not want to take the time or trouble to eat around the pit? Does it take too long? Is it too much trouble?

Or, I hate to think it, but a reasonable conclusion in this litigious society is that the olive sellers simply refuse to take the risk that someone will bite into an olive pit, damage a tooth, and sue the producer, the processor, the distributor, the jar manufacturer, the label printer, and the grocery store, and the poor check-out clerk for millions of dollars, which suit they will most certainly win here in the *Land of the Free and Home of the Brave Litigant*. Call me cynical, but whenever I think I might be too cynical I am made aware of some government or legal or social stupidity that tells me I'm not yet cynical enough.

Writing:

In an earlier Chapter I made mention of letting go of Prozac. My doctor, many years ago when he prescribed it, told me that it was a "serotonin re-uptake inhibitor;" its purpose in life was to inhibit the re-absorption of serotonin by those evil nerve endings that were supposed to pass it along so that the chemical could be transmitted to and picked up by other nerve endings so it could be useful to me. In my system, that serotonin was being re-absorbed by the sending nerve endings which refused to share it. (Selfish bastards!) The result being that I didn't receive the benefit of this chemical in my brain. In short, I was depressed because of a chemical shortage or imbalance. I read an article by another doctor that said this was all theory proposed by the manufacturer and was probably BS.

I have no idea. All I know is that a former significant other didn't want me on the drug. She said it made me a walking zombie (minus the appetite for brains). I know it prohibited me from feeling the lows and exhibiting the attached behaviors that went along with them, but it also constructed a firm ceiling against any highs and being able to experience or express anything resembling extreme happiness or joy. My emotions ran the gamut from M to N; A to L and O to Z were somewhere, locked deep inside. My anti-depressant regimen kept a lot of negative emotions in check at the expense of any positive emotions that might cause me to resemble a human being.

With that said, there has always been something inside of me that wants desperately to get out through some artistic expression – through writing, music, something else? I have no idea what it is or how I should express it. An artist allows what's inside to get out, to be expressed through some medium. I'd love to be an artist. But I'd built an edifice around myself as impregnable as the Great Wall of China or the Alhambra. Whatever is in here was not going to see the light of day no matter what my spirit wanted. The pressure was unbearable, but I had developed the strength to withhold every sign of emotion like Arnold Schwarzenegger developed his lats. Nothing was getting out no matter how much pressure built up inside. And Prozac was my partner in crime.

So I quit.

What I found was that I was suddenly and without warning an emotional basket case. Over the course of their lives people usually develop mechanisms for dealing with emotions and normally keep them in check when not socially appropriate. For twenty years, while on Prozac, I hadn't had to deal with any emotional extremes and apparently I'd completely forgotten what they felt like and, more importantly, how to manage them in polite company. Suddenly it was if all those emotions had been trapped inside me and without Mr. Prozac as gatekeeper they were free to leave the zoo, to run wild, unchecked like a herd of wildebeests running through the Serengeti.

On the Camino I was able to experience feelings of joy, happiness, extreme contentment such as I had never felt. But as I neared Santiago and saw the end of a near-nirvana experience, the closest thing to heaven I had ever experienced, or could imagine ever experiencing in the future, an incredible, unearthly sadness would overcome me and I would fall apart. I remember sitting at a table in an albergue after dinner with my new-found Camino amigos just a few days from Finisterre, and feeling such a weight of melancholy overcome me that I could not contain myself, wracked with inexpressible grief, crying uncontrollably. One of the side effects of quitting Prozac is that one cries a lot. I'm the poster boy for the Prozac-withdrawal crowd. I think about the Camino and I cry. I think about the friends I left in Spain and I cry. I think about my children – how proud of them I am, and I cry, or how I hurt for them because they didn't have a father worthy of them as they grew up, and I cry. I have to intentionally keep myself from thinking or discussing certain subjects with people even a year after I weaned myself off the drug lest I break down into an uncontrollable basket case.

The reason I decided to write this memoir was that I thought if I expressed my feelings about the experience, let the emotions out, that I would be able to get to a point where the feelings weren't a burden to me and could be transformed into, if not happy, at least pleasant memories. But I can't be satisfied with a newspaper report, just writing where I went and how sore my feet were, like Sargent Friday's end-of-day report, "Just the facts, ma'am." I need artistic expression. I want you, the reader, to feel what I felt and see what I saw, to understand why those were the best fifty days of my life.

On the recommendation of one of my dearest friends I bought and started reading *Eat, Pray, Love* by Elizabeth Gilbert. Listen to her poetry in her description of ushering in the New Year at an ashram in India:

> *As the minutes pass, it feels to me like we are collectively pulling the year 2004 toward us. Like we have roped it with our music, and now we are hauling it across the night sky like it's a massive fishing net, brimming with all our unknown destinies. And what a heavy net it is, indeed, carrying as it does all the births, deaths, tragedies, wars, love stories, inventions, transformations, and calamities that are destined for all of us this coming year. We keep singing and we keep hauling, hand-over-hand, minute-by-minute, voice after voice, closer and closer. The seconds drop down to midnight and we sing with our biggest effort yet and in this last brave exertion we finally pull the net of New Year over us, covering both the sky and ourselves with it. God only knows what the year might contain, but now it is here, and we are all beneath it.*

That's not the best paragraph in the book; I just pulled it out at random. Almost every sentence in the book is a gold mine of word painting. I read the first three chapters of that book and was reduced to tears in my neighborhood Starbucks. I had to leave before finishing my latte. I wanted to give up writing this little memoir. Why bother? Everything I could possibly say about life's struggles or self-discovery has already been said, and said so much better than I could possibly think of even attempting. Ms. Gilbert paints with words like Caravaggio painted with oils and colors. I feel her feelings. I see the streets of Italy and the cow paths of India that she traverses. I taste her gelato in Rome and pizza in Sicily. I feel her frustrations to the depths of my soul as she goes through divorce and then loses the love of her life on top of that. I weep with her and I celebrate her accomplishments because she writes so damn well. She invites me into her life and I cry and laugh and rejoice with her and then I curse God for giving me the will and the need to express myself through some sort of art, any art, but then not giving me the talent for anything except building tremendously thick, impregnable walls against everyone, walls that keep inside anything that might be worth sharing with the outside world.

No, I'm not on Ms. Gilbert's payroll. Great art is everywhere and in uncountable forms. I discovered my love of literature in John Steinbeck; every sentence of his that I read pierces my heart. Or listen to Pavarotti sing a Puccini aria, or take an hour and look at Picasso's Guernica if you happen to be in Madrid. Great art is all around us and it will change you if you let it.

And no, I don't literally curse God. I know every struggle I have is part of a learning process and series of tests I have to go through in this life. I have a strong belief that we have a soul which goes through many lives on Earth as a child goes through many days of school between kindergarten and a Ph.D. We can't learn everything in one brief life and we can't just sail through life with no challenges. What would be the point? I know my frustrations are just learning opportunities and tests. But even Jesus had doubts and he was a perfect being, an ascended master. If he had doubts, can't I?

I'll keep writing as a means of searching for meaning of my experience in Spain, walking the Camino de Santiago between Montserrat and Finisterre, meeting other pilgrims and falling in love with one in particular, simultaneously enjoying and enduring, ascending to a place between heaven and Earth and then having to return to a mundane life and wondering, "What the hell was that all about?" Maybe I'll find the answer to that question in this life, or maybe I'll have to wait until class is over when I'll finally get to sit with my spirit teachers to review this life's lessons.

But when presented with what a master can do with the same words I have to work with, and having seen what's possible compared with my meager attempts, it's sometimes difficult to continue. It's just an unfortunate circumstance that we're inspired by the best that the world has to offer – Beethoven, Steinbeck, Pavarotti, Renoir, Adams – and then as we develop our own talents we naturally compare ourselves against those who inspired us in the first place, and most of us find ourselves falling short of the standards we've set for ourselves.

But it's been said that if you give a million monkeys a million typewriters, in a million years one of them is going to produce another Shakespeare play. Call me conceited, but I consider myself better than a monkey with a typewriter, so there's still hope.

Logroño

June 9th

I arrived in Logroño not knowing what to expect, but as that had been the norm every day on the Camino, that was fine – no, more than fine by me. I looked forward to every day, to every adventure, to the heat, the silence, the sore feet, to the constantly changing vistas, the personality of every pueblo and city I passed through. I'm not a very social person, but now that I was joining the French route where there would be more pilgrims, I wondered if I would meet other people and learn their stories, why they were here, where they had been, learn of their experiences, their successes and disappointments. I wondered if I were the only one with foot problems, the only one who was looking for a complete change of life. I figured that many other people making such a grueling, long walk would also have heart-felt and serious reasons for doing so. What surprised me was the number of people I met who were there purely for the fun of it, who had made the journey multiple times before. I learned that everyone had his own Camino, which, in Spanish translates to the English *path,* and in this case translates very well as that word: We were all on our own *path*, whether it be physical, spiritual, or both combined. If there are a thousand people on the Camino, there are a thousand reasons for being there. I found, though, that those of a like mind tended to find each other and form a small, albeit, unfortunately temporary group of traveling companions.

This was to be the first city with more than one albergue, and the first albergue I spent the night in where I would be one of who knows how many people enjoying the accommodations. For the first time on the Camino, I stood in line to register at an albergue, but was glad to find that the cost was only seven euros. My time of forty to fifty euros per day seemed to be at an end. But then again, so were my days of sleeping in a quiet room sans snoring. As with all of life, there is good and bad, yin and yang. Thank heaven for ear plugs is all I can say.

Another surprise: this albergue had washing machines for clothes. I had been hand-washing my clothes for weeks and I don't mind saying I was downright ecstatic for this little modern convenience. I sat in the albergue's courtyard, feet in the cold pool of a fountain, drinking a semi-cold beer from their vending machine (Beer from a vending machine! Is this a great country or what?!), and waiting for my clothes to be washed automatically! Yes, I had enjoyed my solo time walking through Catalunya and Aragon, but joining the crowd and inexpensive albergues prepared for them had its benefits.

Later I walked through the nearby environs of Logroño, which, coincidentally, was host this particular weekend to a regional celebration. Logroño is the capital city of *La Rioja* and I was fortunate enough to be there during what might be called their "founders' days." This was a first on the Camino – it was actually difficult to find a place to eat. There were thousands upon thousands of people everywhere, in every bar, every restaurant, filling to capacity every square.

I was looking forward to Logroño where I thought I would be able to buy a power converter and a couple of cotton T-shirts. I found that the expensive, wick-away-the-sweat (baloney!) synthetic shirts I had bought at the high-end outdoor stores were uncomfortable in the heat and I longed for a simple, natural cotton T-shirt. But, as this was a festival weekend in Spain, everything except restaurants was closed. Thousands upon thousands of people, including tourists, in the street and not a shop open to buy anything. Spaniards take their festivals seriously. What's the use of having a festival if you have to work? Who am I to judge? All I knew was that I couldn't spend my money for anything except food and alcohol.

Amidst the throngs of people I couldn't find any place to have a normal dinner so I ended up just having some *tapas* after elbowing my way in to a couple of bars, including a wonderful duck paté, with a couple of glasses of the best wine I had had so far on the Camino (and it was only a *crianza*!). As I walked back to the albergue I passed another bar whose *tapas* looked so good I had to stop for more. I didn't make any notes about this in my journal but more than nine months later I still remember the sensations of flavors – savory meats, patés, cheeses, and seafood on crusty bread or just served plain on a plate, mixtures of tastes that I never would have expected to find together but seemed to be created for each other once I got over the surprise of finding them cohabitating on the same piece of bread.

I hadn't yet found God, but I finally found those great Spanish *tapas* I had been looking for in Logroño.

The last picture before Logroño, where my camino was to change dramatically.

Ventosa and Camino Amigos

June 10th

I'm finding it difficult to write Part Two, where I meet other people leaving Logroño, one of whom becomes an integral part of my Camino experience. Before this point I could write what I saw, what I did, a little of how I felt, and it was all just me, all the time, every day. From here, though, much of my Camino experience is wrapped up with other people whose privacy I will be invading and much deeper feelings I will have to reveal if I'm going to write honestly. I think it was Camus who said "A work of art is a confession." Whether I'm creating a work of art is in the eye of the beholder, but there are definitely elements of confession here. If I'm less than completely forthcoming it's only to protect the privacy of those who have no say in what I'm writing.

I had to start using my ear plugs in Logroño. I was in a room of about a dozen bunk beds – twenty-four men – so you can imagine the snoring. As if that weren't enough, the celebration outside lasted until at least 2:00 AM. Lights-out at the albergue was 10:00 PM and I was tired as usual, so sleep came easily. But about the time I'd get near dreamland I'd be awoken by either snoring or the fiesta occurring outside. This went on until the wee hours of the morning when I finally found that deep, restful sleep I craved and needed. When I awoke, I found that I was the only person in the room; everyone else had gotten up and was on the road. With my earplugs and the efforts of other pilgrims' to move about as quietly as possible so as not to disturb the others who preferred to sleep, the room full of twenty-three other men preparing their back packs and getting dressed was more conducive to sleep than had been the revelers in the streets some blocks away and the snoring through the night. This became the norm for the rest of the Camino. I had no schedule, which was one of the absolute beauties of the experience, and at this time of year there didn't seem to be any danger of there being no place left to sleep in any pueblo in which I stopped for the night (save one or two times, noted later), so I was never dependent upon an alarm to wake up.

As it turned out, that was one of the most fortunate circumstances of my Camino because as I left the albergue I fell into step with a few other late starters passing by who had stayed the night at another albergue: Maria and Beth from Catalunya, Adolfo from Valencia, Diego from Málaga, and Annick from France. I had written some post cards to send home to friends and family and asked the group if they knew where a post box might be. As we seemed to be walking at roughly the same tempo, I continued walking with them through Logroño and beyond. We didn't walk the entire remainder of the Camino together, and several days later we lost Diego and Adolfo, but for the most part, my Camino memories from Logroño to Finisterre are intertwined with, and mean very little without, Maria, Beth, and Annick. I miss them so much now it is difficult to write this.

Maria told me some weeks later that the four of them – she, Beth, Adolfo, and Diego – were trying that first few hours after meeting me to figure out who I was. They were sure that I was an American movie star, but they couldn't quite place me. I smile every time I think of that. I'm sure the same thing happened to Shirley MacLaine all the time. Shirley and I – we have a lot in common.

Me, doing my movie star imitation somewhere West of Logroño. I looked more "movie-starish" when I was wearing my Ray Bans. The "evening shoes," hanging from my pack by this time were worthless – they fit when I started, but not now.

Walking alongside Diego I got some excellent Spanish practice as he told me all about the challenges of his local *futbol* (soccer) team and the beauties of Málaga. He talked at around 60 miles an hour, with gusts up to 90. That first day I think I caught about 30 to 40 percent of what he said, but by the end of the second day walking with him I was beginning to feel pretty good about my Spanish, understanding better than 75 percent, in my estimation. Thinking back, that may have been an optimistic guess; there were many times later where I thought I had understood what was being said, only to find out I had missed something germane to the conversation which more than once caused me some embarrassment when my lack of understanding came back to bite me.

That first day we only walked to Ventosa, although the guide suggested walking on to Najera, another 10 kilometers further along. However, the albergue in Najera only had fourteen spaces and, as we had gotten a late start, we didn't want to take the chance that it might be full by the time we got there and the next option was another six kilometers. Nope, not going to do that. We took it easy and stopped.

I'm glad we did because the *Albergue San Saturnino* is one of the nicest on the entire Camino. The hostess, or *hospitalera*, was extremely pleasant and helpful. The albergue had recently been completely remodeled with very comfortable beds, a nice patio, washing machine and dryer, and music that exactly suited my tastes, which, I might add, are excellent. (ha!) The *hospitalera* was playing Miles Davis when we arrived and we awoke the following morning to Gregorian Chant. I thought I had died and gone to heaven. I didn't want to get out of bed, but the Camino was calling and pilgrims aren't allowed to stay more than one night at an albergue, no matter how good the music.

Diego, Annick, Adolfo, 2 pilgrims from Japan at the near side of the table and an unidentified pilgrim relaxing in the courtyard of the Albergue San Saturnino

Azofra to Redecilla del Camino

June 11th-13th

I wish now that I had written more in my journal, but I was simply enjoying the Camino and the truth is, I went with the intention of only doing each day what my heart told me to do. I wrote when I felt like it, but didn't consider it an obligation. I hardly made any notes of my thoughts or the things that happened along the way; I didn't want the time spent annotating the experience to decrease the time I had to simply experience the experience. Further, honestly, I had no intention of writing a memoir. My Camino was to be a completely private and, frankly, self-centered experience. The writing is only to work through some emotions and hopefully release them through some sort of expression so that I can get past the PTSD brick wall that keeps me from enjoying my memories.

And there's the other thing: I had been walking in silence for the last three weeks, listening for some word from God, for some revelation, or at least a good joke or two. I wanted relief from the same old daily thoughts I'd had for decades, which had all been about my shortcomings and failures, things I was embarrassed about or even ashamed of. There were a few hours of mulling over the problems of the world, but the days, even here on the Camino, for the most part were spent cataloging my deficiencies and how I had hurt people I loved and how I had come up short in every area of my life. I didn't want to write that down. What if I died of heat stroke or was kidnapped or got carried away by one of those giant storks that were as common here as mosquitoes in Minnesota? What if someone discovered an empty pair of boots and my journal laying there on the Camino, and happened to read what I had written? No, better to leave myself a mystery so they would think "That poor soul, part of some stork's nest," rather than "Good riddance, buddy."

So I didn't write much.

On the 11th we got to Azofra. On the 12th we passed through Cirueña, Santo Domingo de la Calzada, and intended to stop in Grañon, but the albergue turned out to be just an upper room in a 12th century church – no running water, no little kitchenette with a microwave, no beds. We'd be sleeping on a stone floor and bathing in the outdoor fountain. I had my comfortable air mattress and had spent a few nights in albergues with only a sink with cold water, so brushing my teeth and washing my face in the fountain in the town square was OK with me. The others, though, thought the effort of walking the extra four kilometers would be energy well spent. I was enjoying the company of my new-found friends and even though my feet were saying "STOP!" I was not about to stay in Grañon while they went ahead, with the possibility of never seeing them again.

So we walked another four kilometers to Redecilla del Camino, Beth singing and laughing and making jokes in Catalan of which I understood exactly *nada*, Maria helping me with my Spanish as I tried to carry on a rudimentary conversation, correcting often and laughing just as much when I'd refer to myself in the feminine form of noun or pronoun, which I seemed to do a lot. Annick walked mostly in silence, but we conversed a little, as she was fairly fluent in English. We had lost Adolfo and Diego earlier when they took a detour, intending to meet up with us later but we seemed to have missed the rendezvous. We never saw them again.

The night of June 11th it rained hard so we walked through deep mud the next morning between Azofra and Cirueña. I felt awful for Beth because she only had sandals on her feet; the boots she had originally brought turned out to not fit well and she had to leave them behind well before Logroño. She began the Camino on a whim, originally planning to walk with Maria only a few days, but as each day passed she decided to walk another day, then another, until finally deciding to continue all the way to Santiago. She was not adequately prepared and had severe problems with blisters on her feet the entire way, but kept walking when I would have stayed in a hotel soaking my feet. Not only did she keep walking, but she kept singing. She must have known the words to every popular song on the radio. And she kept smiling and laughing. And all the while each of her feet were a colony of blisters that I knew from painful experience were killing her. I carried a well-equipped first aid kit and each night I'd help her care for her feet as much as she'd let me. (The truth is, and I'm sure Beth wouldn't mind my saying, that she is a complete wimp when it comes to lancing a blister.) On the one hand I wanted to tell her, "Look, you're not prepared for this. Call it a day and go home. Come back next year when you've had the chance to prepare yourself with the proper clothing and equipment." On the other hand, I wanted to pick her up and carry her, do anything I could to help. The strength of here spirit was unbelievable and an encouragement to me. No foot pain I was experiencing compared to what she was going through every single day on the Camino. We got separated and I lost track of her the last week or so of the Camino. She eventually had to slow down and stayed extra days at some albergues to give her feet a little extra time to heal. I think of Beth often and miss her, as I miss all of my Camino Amigos.

Between Azofra to Cirueña the morning after the rain.

Maria

June 13th

Leaving Redecilla, my camino amigos and I walked through Castildelgado, Viloria, Villamayor del Río, Belorado, Tosantos, Villambistia, Espinosa del Camino, Villafranca, and finally stopped for the night at Montes de Oca. The rain had stopped. The weather was perfect. The company was better.

On June 14th we stopped in Atapuerca. It was a short day but everyone had sore feet and it just seemed like a good idea, especially since the following day we'd have another relatively short and easy walk to Burgos where we planned to stay an extra day for rest and relaxation. We walked through beautiful, cool forests, albeit with some fairly steep terrain. My guide book said we climbed about 400 meters before heading down again. That doesn't sound like much to an *Americano*, used to measuring in feet, but that's a climb of about 400 yards, or 1,200 feet. It's not mountain climbing by any stretch of the imagination, but it's good exercise for the quads and lungs, and the walk down was equally hard on the toes and knees. I'm not complaining, mind you; The First Rule of the Pilgrim is "Don't complain."

I think it was at about this time that I started thinking that if I ever did anything like this again it would be with a pair of custom-made boots, no matter how much they cost. If I were to complain (and I wouldn't, of course) it would only be about one thing, and that was my feet. The best-fitting off-the-shelf boots I found, with custom orthotic inserts, still bent at the wrong place and weren't wide enough or long enough in the toes. The entire sole of my foot ached at the end of each day, my toes were jammed into the front of my boots, especially walking down hill, and my little toes were bent under the toe next to them all day long, causing pain and blisters. This was all manageable on Saturday training walks of 12 Km before the Camino, with a week to rest in between hikes. But subjecting my feet to a daily routine of 25 to 35 Km., some days more, without time to recuperate was taking a toll. I know I've written about this ad infinitum, but that's what was on my mind each day as I'd walk. In preparation for my next saunter I have already bought a pair of custom boots from *Esatto Custom Hiking Boots* in Battleground, Washington. We'll see how they fare. I still have flat, misshapen feet, but I'm hoping for a much better foot experience between Barcelona and Rome in 2015.

It was at this stage, as the little group of people composed of Annick, Beth, Maria and I neared Burgos, that I fell in love with Maria. In my defense, anyone who spent time with Maria and got to know her even just a little would fall in love with her. I wasn't the only one. Between Logroño and Finisterre we walked together roughly two thirds of the time, maybe a little more. There would be hours in the day, sometimes days in the week, where we'd become separated, walking alone or with other groups of people. When that would happen and I'd stop for a rest, people with whom I became acquainted along the Camino would ask about her. If I was asked once, I was asked a hundred times, "Where's Maria?" Everyone enjoyed her company. They wanted to be around her. Everyone was uplifted and energized by her. Maria made everyone feel a little bit better just being in her company. She had an aura that radiated good energy, enveloping people, uplifting their tired spirits. She had a smile and a positive word for everyone. Those who were tired, in pain, feeling frustrated or exhausted were less so after a few minutes in Maria's presence. A healing, generous, joyful energy surrounded her.

How do you not love someone who volunteers as one of a troupe of clowns that visits terminally ill children to give them a little laughter and happiness? How do you not love someone who goes on aid missions to South America, living for months in a mud hut without even running water? Maria isn't what we'd call a bleeding-heart liberal. She doesn't tell other people how they should live; she just goes about living her life, her convictions. She speaks through her actions, and her actions demonstrate everything that is good about humans.

Later, I was to encounter a photography exhibit in an upper room of an ancient church in a tiny pueblo. Some of the photographs had a poem or phrase with them; a thought, a prayer. One I remember in particular said,

> While I slept, I dreamed that life was happiness.
> When I awoke, I found that life was service.
> When I served, I learned that service was happiness.

I believe that was written with Maria in mind.

There were times when Maria wasn't perfectly happy and content. She had her challenges and dealt with issues the same as everyone else. She didn't talk about them, but in conversation, little things would be said in passing that gave me small bits of information that I put together which told me that she had ghosts haunting her no less than anyone else. But her aura was too strong for them to get close or to remain in her vicinity for very long. She repelled sadness and pain, and all those around her benefited from her multi-hued energy shield.

Sitting in the cathedral in Montserrat May 20th, listening to vespers, I prayed that I would be led on a journey of discovery, that I would advance spiritually on this trek, this saunter, that I would be shown miracles and wonders, that my life would be changed on the Camino. I talked with my guardian angels along the way, asking for guidance and praying that whatever experiences were in store for me on the Camino, I would take notice of and realize for their benefit to enrich and improve my life, that I would use them to make myself a better person. I didn't know why I was led to begin my Camino in the unusual location of Montserrat, and why I had such problems with my feet that I had to stop for two extra days of rest in Lleída and Zaragoza. But because I started in Montserrat and took exactly twenty days to reach Logroño and slept late the morning I left that city and had written post cards and didn't know where to mail them, and had to ask a group of strangers as I left the albergue if they knew where I might find a post box, I met Maria. I can't quantify, and it's difficult to qualify, how my Camino experience was changed by that chance meeting. But I can't imagine what the remaining several hundred kilometers of the Camino would have been like without Maria's presence.

An Embarrassment of Riches

June 15th

We arrived in Burgos, walking through a bucolic city park filled with runners and parents walking their children in strollers on a path along a meandering river. The weather was perfect; sun shining, not too hot, not too cool, no wind. I was reminded of the painting, *Sunday in the Park* by Georges Seurat.

Entering Burgos through the park

It had been a short day of walking and we entered the city at mid-afternoon with plenty of time to find lodging, rest, and have a leisurely dinner. I had planned to stay in an inexpensive hotel since we'd be there a couple of days and albergues allow only one night unless you're having physical problems that preclude your leaving. That, and I wanted to get a couple of nights' sleep in a big bed between sheets (no sleeping bag) without earplugs and enjoy a long, hot shower or two. It wasn't a pilgrim experience, I admit, but sometimes you have to go with the flow and do as the spirit tells you. The spirit was telling me to relax and enjoy myself. I did, and felt thoroughly blessed.

Sadly, Annick had decided to jump ahead on the Camino, taking a bus to Leon the next afternoon, as she was running out of time. She had begun in Le Puy, France and so had already been on her Camino for about forty days by the time she reached Saint Jean Pied de Port, where most pilgrims begin. This would be her last night with us as a little group of pilgrims – she, Maria, Beth, and I – so I wanted us all to have a special dinner together and invited them to join me and allow me to buy dinner for everyone. (I was pretending to be a rich American, I suppose.) After finding a hotel and while wandering the town I had seen a restaurant called "Godfather" with a menu of Italian food (as you'd expect) that looked good and was decorated in the theme of the movie by that name. The Godfather in Burgos? Sounds funny, but it worked.

We were on pilgrim time, which meant that dinner started no later than 8:00 because albergue doors normally close at 10:00 PM. On the Camino, if you're not in the albergue by 10:00 PM you have to find someplace else to sleep. Even if you've already checked in, claimed a bed, and deposited your pack and other gear, the doors are locked at 10:00. However, in normal Spanish culture and cities, not purely disposed to cater to pilgrims, as are a lot of small pueblos we passed through, an 8:00 dinner is early so we were virtually the first people there.

I was correct: The food was excellent, as was the service (no *mala folla* here!) and the wine was better, made even more so by the price. I ordered a wine I was familiar with that would have easily cost $70 to $80 at an American restaurant that was only 20 euros at Godfather. I've said it before but it bears repeating: Is Spain a great country or what? We had a wonderful four-course meal, Maria and I sharing an absolutely delicious chocolate crepe for desert that could have served the whole table, but we ate it all ourselves.

Sometime during the desert course, Maria and Beth noted with some excitement a man sitting at the next table, surrounded by three gorgeous women. Turns out he was someone famous in Spanish television, host to some celebrity gossip show. I couldn't remember his name if my life depended on it, but soon the restaurant was abuzz and people were having a difficult time not looking at him. Many were staring, not even attempting to display some sense of reserve. (I like to imagine that the citizens of my adopted country are above that sort of behavior, so I'm going to allow myself to believe that the gawkers must have been tourists.) Presently, there were people at the windows of the restaurant taking flash pictures. After dinner Maria and Beth stopped to say hello. "Mr. Famous" was very friendly with them: no surprise there. Like I said, everyone instantly likes Maria and Beth also has a very warm personality. They talked for quite a while as Annick and I waited outside and, I found out later, he actually invited them to join him and his small harem of beautiful women for the rest of the night. One of the women in his entourage quickly nixed the idea and Maria and Beth politely declined.

I was happy they did because we spent the rest of the night and early morning hours, until about 4:30 AM, in various bars sampling the night life of Burgos. Again, I have nothing good to say about the techno-crap music that's common in Spain, but I really didn't care. I was pretending to be much younger, a much better dancer, and much more of a party animal than I am in real life. This is not standard pilgrim behavior, but as I said, I was following the spirits (that would be alcohol spirits in this case) and I had the time of my life.

The next day we wandered around town, separately during the morning, and then met up in the afternoon to tour the cathedral.

The Cathedral of Burgos

The Cathedral of Burgos has to be one of the most beautiful, most amazing, awe-inspiring cathedrals in the world. It was constructed over the course of more than three centuries, requiring literally millions of man hours and incalculable money to build, and then restore some centuries later. It is still in a state of restoration today. The day I visited the cathedral it was gleaming white against a crystal blue sky overlaid with wispy white clouds that were embarrassed by the gracefulness and shear magnificence of the spires of the cathedral.

And I was almost ashamed to call myself a follower of Jesus.

A tiny portion of the Cathedral of Burgos

We toured the cathedral with recorders in hand, listening to descriptions in our native languages of the various chapels and naves, the architecture, the art, and the unabashed hubris of the bishops through the centuries who spent the people's tithes on monuments to their pride. Somewhere, over in the corner of the cathedral was a chapel for Jesus, small and relatively modest, while the rest of the cathedral was a collection of chapels constructed around a bishop's marble coffin in the middle, and an alter surrounded by marble carvings and frescoes, normally with his family members and maybe a mistress or two as models for the personages in the art.

I understand the meaning of beauty in the House of the Lord and its use in bringing to the worshiper a sense of awe in His presence, a sense of His power that inspires humans to design and create such structures. I felt inspired and blessed in the cathedral in Montserrat, but at some point there are limits, and the Cathedral of Burgos surpasses those limits by more than I could have imagined. The same art, sculpture, arching space, marble and granite, without the monuments in each chapel to the bishops who controlled the church at various periods through the centuries required to build the cathedral might be inspiring. But I couldn't get past the bishops' pride that was so obviously the motivation for its building. I've been in awe-inspiring mosques that, by Muslim law, do not allow images of God (Allah), much less that of an imam or other persons who may have taken part in or motivated its construction. They are truly beautiful works of art and eschew human pride. Like a slap upside the head, I had a sudden and powerful awakening to how a Muslim might view the world of Christendom in ages past and even now, and I would have a difficult time arguing with him. I left that monument to pride feeling completely "cathedraled out." I didn't visit another until I reached Santiago.

The famous mosque of Cordoba. No bishop's pride in sight.

The next morning I awoke to the sound of the mobile phone I carried with me for emergencies. Maria and Beth had stayed in a pension to save money, rather than in the hotel I chose for myself. Maria was calling to tell me she wanted to walk a while by herself. While I completely understood, having had almost three weeks to myself earlier, of which I enjoyed every minute, I have to admit that I was somewhat saddened (bummed out is how I really felt) by her decision.

As I've mentioned, she was a very special person and added something to the Camino experience that I missed when she wasn't around. But I put on my pack and began walking alone again – the wrong way – out of Burgos. Luckily I saw a couple of other pilgrims walking the right way so I only went a few blocks before turning around and finding a yellow arrow and the Camino for another day of solo sauntering.

West of Burgos. The Camino continues

Who Are These Pilgrims?

Looking for something on the web, I forget what, I came across *The Holy Rover Blog* and an article about *"Walking the Country as a Spiritual Quest."* The author references an article from *The New York Times* by Kate Murphy from which she quotes this paragraph:

> *Anthropologists have long argued that pilgrims occupy a so-called liminal realm outside of, yet proximal to, society. "In this space you can achieve a direct human interaction that doesn't take into account hierarchies, so people become intimate very quickly," said Ellen Badone, author of* Intersecting Journeys: The Anthropology of Pilgrimage and Tourism *and professor of anthropology and religious studies at McMaster University in Hamilton, Ontario. "Stepping into this extraordinary sphere leads to* **extraordinary interactions where you very quickly become close and find that people are willing to go out of their way to be helpful***"* (emphasis mine).

That is exactly what I found on the Camino de Santiago. Should I be relieved or disappointed to find that this is just normal human behavior? I wanted to believe that the Camino de Santiago is somehow special, that it attracts a different and wholly unique person: helpful, friendly, positive, willing to interact with and help anyone and everyone on a level not found in "the real world" and that there is some spiritual force on the Camino that envelopes people and enables the best behavior humans can muster. Now I read that people in general who make this type of pilgrimage are, as a whole, cut from the same cloth. The article speaks of people who have walked the breadth of the United States who have found the same peace and sense of wonder, a sense of being human, of being deeply touched by mundane events and finding that the people they meet as they walk really are more interesting and engaging than their Facebook profiles might suggest.

The article also quotes Rebecca Solnit, author of *Wanderlust: A History of Walking*. She says, "*Part of the desire to do it* (make a pilgrimage) *is to accept that the world is unpredictable and you will trust what the world sends your way and you will cope with it.*" Again, this is exactly what I felt, and what everyone I met on the Camino also seemed to believe.

As I contemplate and plan my next pilgrimage, Barcelona to Rome, I have a nagging sense of fear in the far recesses of my mind that the experience will be disappointing, that the happiness and contentment I found on the Camino de Santiago was a high point in my life that I'll never again attain. Then I read the words above and feel encouraged. Perhaps my next pilgrimage might bring a sense of happiness equal to that which I felt on the Camino de Santiago.

Hope springs eternal.

Hontanas and Boadilla del Camino

June 17th

I walked the entire day solo, again, as in "the old days." It wasn't bad, I suppose. I didn't have to exercise my Spanish brain cells, except to order food and drink for lunch, but that was old hat now – no effort needed. I had the day to think, feel, observe; or not think, not feel, not observe. It was a little odd. It had only been a few days since I'd left my solo experience, walking with others, and I was already in the rhythm of walking with a group. Maybe I'm more of a social animal than I thought. Or maybe, I really liked the people I was walking with and as I've noted before, Maria had an aura that radiated energy and good feelings and Beth was always laughing and singing. Walking with them, the days just went by a little faster.

Hanging laundry in the albergue built in the ruins of an ancient convent

I arrived in Hontanas, a very small pueblo. My guide book said there was only one albergue, San Anton, in the ruins of an ancient convent. In that albergue there are no electric lights, so the only light after sunset is by candle. However there was another albergue, not listed in the guide book, which I chose – modern, comfortable, with washing machines and a small kitchen. I caught up with Maria and Beth there, but didn't spend much time with them as Maria had expressed her intent to spend some days alone and I honored her wishes. I helped Beth with her feet, with much grumbling and whining on her part; but I did the best she would allow. I like to help where I can. That's what pilgrims do. It just kind of comes naturally.

After I ate dinner I wandered down to an ancient church and found there was a photography exhibit in an upper room. A photographer and a man she had met on the Camino on a previous pilgrimage created an absolutely awe-inspiring collection of photographs and texts that went with each that captured a spirit of the Camino I hadn't found up to that point. The words and photographs caused an awakening in me. The photographs were nothing short of masterful and the words were inspiring, thought-provoking, and sometimes emotionally wrenching. The photographer/writer had a way of tearing your heart out, ripping it to shreds, then reforming it better than before and handing it back to you with a photograph and a few words. I left her exhibit seeing, feeling, and experiencing the Camino in a completely different way. I had been through some of the same places she had photographed but I hadn't seen what she captured in her camera. I looked back on those places and now saw them, thought about them, thought about the whole experience of the Camino in a different light. The photographs affected how I saw and experienced my pilgrimage, past as well as future. As much as Maria had changed, and was changing, my Camino, these words and photographs also gave me a completely different perspective on my journey not only across northern Spain, but my entire life.

I wish I could tell you the name of the photographer and quote some of the texts, other than that quoted a couple of chapters ago. I bought a small book of the photographs with the texts that I unfortunately sent back to the States sometime later to save weight in my pack and, as I've written in an earlier chapter, the box was opened in transit and a few things were stolen from it. The book of photographs was one of the things taken. I've searched the web to try to find a site the photographer might have created, but to date have not found it.

Inside the albergue in Boadilla del Camino

The next day, June 19th, I walked to Boadilla del Camino where there is one of the nicest albergues on the Camino, complete with a small swimming pool. The weather wasn't warm enough to swim, but it felt great to put my hot, tired feet in the pool until they were numb. I had completed almost a month on the Camino, settling in to a peaceful routine and getting quite used to a life I could have continued forever, or at least another 40 or 50 years. If it weren't for the necessity to beg for food and lodging, I could easily see how the life of a wandering vagabond would be very appealing: Time to think, time to feel, time to see, to experience the best that people are – helpful, kind, giving, not judging, sharing pain and joy openly and without reservation. On the web in "social networks" (and I use that term loosely) where people are anonymous or at least physically separated from everyone else, they feel free to be themselves, to express whatever they are thinking, or not be themselves, to develop alter-egos, someone they might like to be, acting without the filters of social mores inhibiting them. On the Camino, people are also free to be themselves, but they are *themselves,* their <u>real</u> selves, open and honest, with the addition of a physical presence which makes all the difference.

Oracion de la Amistad

A friendship Prayer

Jesucristo Maestro y amigo, damos la ruta por un mundo de odios y rencores. Nos de miedo la soledad. Queremos ir en compaña: protege nuestra amistad. Busca entre nosotros confianza total. Ayúdanos a superar el rencor y la duda. Danos un corazón para comprender y ayudar a todos los demás.

Jesus Christ, our lord and friend, show us the way through a world of hate and rancor. We are fearful of solitude. We want to be in your company and under your protection. Find in us complete confidence. Help us to overcome rancor and doubt. Give us a heart to understand and help all others.

This was another prayer I saw, written in three languages, on a wall along the road we were walking one day. Things like this, receiving help, encouragement, various little gifts of all kinds were common. I suppose this is one of the things that makes returning to the "real world" so difficult. It's not as if one never receives help and kindness from strangers outside of the Camino, but it's rare; It's not a day-to-day, quotidian event. It's easy to forget that we're all in this together when we're rushing to and from work, taking the kids to soccer practice, trying to balance work with relationships. On the Camino, work, traffic, soccer practice, conflicting

146

obligations, and the rest of the world's distractions are far away, over the horizon, on the other side of the ocean. The pilgrim has the time and the luxury to be in the moment, to enjoy solitude or relationships as he chooses. The only obligation is simply to be and continue walking each day. It's a magical place, a place that doesn't exist in the real world, at least not in a world that I've ever experienced outside of the Camino.

June 19th or 20th. I had lost track of the days; my journal and guidebook relate conflicting dates when I was at the same place. Oh well. *No pasa nada.*

I arrived in Carrion de los Condes and checked in to a large albergue in a convent run by, as you might expect, nuns. It was a well-equipped and large, with two kitchens and a courtyard complete with chairs and tables for outdoor eating and a half basketball court for those who, after a day of walking, still had enough energy to play basketball. (Count me out.)

Maria and Beth had taken a taxi here from Boadilla del Camino because Beth was still having extreme difficulties with blisters on her feet. The next morning Beth decided to stay an extra day at the convent to rest and allow her feet to recuperate a little more. Truth was, her feet needed much more time than just an extra day or two to heal, but she was determined to keep walking. As I think back, having helped Beth with her feet, dressing her blisters, her intention to keep walking was nothing short of heroic. I would have stopped. I don't know how she kept walking, but she did. I went to the bus station for her to get the schedule for the bus to the next stop, Sahagún. The nuns took good care of her while Maria and I continued walking, although she started out a little earlier than I because she wanted some solitude, which I, again, completely understood, but left me feeling a little empty nonetheless.

I got a late start, taking some time to make the arrangements for Beth to stay at the convent and to go to the bus station to get the schedule for her. Things were a little disordered compared with the normal morning routine and it was here that I first left my hat and sunglasses; I had forgotten them in the restaurant where Maria and I had breakfast. We ate and then went to a post office to mail various things we didn't need – I, a pair of shoes I had intended to use for "evening wear" that no longer fit because my feet had swollen, along with the aforementioned book of Camino photographs, and Maria, her camera that she rarely used and a few other small things that were taking unnecessary space in her pack. I realized that I had left my hat and sunglasses in the restaurant so we returned and I was able to retrieve them. Then, at the albergue, discussing the plan for Beth's transportation and where we would meet, I set my hat and sunglasses on one of the beds in the dormitory-style room. The day was cloudy and not too warm, and I was getting a late start so I left somewhat hurriedly. Maria probably would have reminded me to take my hat and glasses, but she had already left. It wasn't until a few hours down the road that I realized I was walking hat-less and sunglass-less. Later, when I caught up with Maria who had a phone that actually worked throughout Spain (mine only worked in the largest cities), she was able to call Beth to ask if she might have noticed my sunglasses on one of the beds in the dormitory room. Sadly, they were nowhere to be found. I assume, and hope, that someone found them who needed a good pair of "antique" Ray-Ban sunglasses. The hat I had bought for 2.50 euros so I wasn't concerned. But the sunglasses were another story.

I try to see a purpose in everything. The sunglasses were a gift from a previous girlfriend, the woman of Spanish descent whom I mentioned way back in the beginning, maybe the first or second chapter of this memoir. They were vintage 1993 or '94, one of the first gifts from her very early in our relationship. Other than memories, the sunglasses were the last remnant of my relationship with her, a relationship I had been trying to get over for a decade. I viewed the loss of the sunglasses as symbolic of the end of that relationship – finally. From here, everything about my life was completely new. I had been reborn with virtually nothing more than my birthday suit and a backpack.

Leaving Carrion de los Condes I learned the meaning of a new word: *desvío*: which my on-line Spanish-English dictionary defines as *detour, alternate, or "long cut, the opposite of short-cut."* That last one is the one I remember. It's a small word, seemingly insignificant in the grand scheme of things, written on a sign as I exited the town. I thought nothing of it, in fact, I'm not sure I even noticed it, but Maria told me later that it was there. No matter now. I followed the arrow that said *"Camino desvío"* and found myself on a busy, ugly, noisy highway for about ten or twelve kilometers. By the time I finally stopped to ask if I was still on the Camino, I found that I had taken a small detour. Why there is a detour from the Camino on a busy highway I'll never know, but after a few hours I came across a welcome sign pointing me back to the normal Camino route and left the noisy highway, happy to be away from the traffic and back to a peaceful walk in the countryside. In the past I would have been upset, angry, full of invective toward myself for taking the wrong route and causing myself extra work. But that's not what I remember feeling. This was just another day on the Camino. I had been lost in a large nature preserve on my first day, later I had been lost in the desert in Aragon. I might get lost again. This was a microcosm of my life. I let it go and continued walking, still enjoying the walk. I met up with the normal Camino route after about an hour and found, much to my surprise and elation, Maria. We walked for a few kilometers but, trying to be respectful of her wish to be alone for a while, I stopped without her at a very comfortable little bar and sat in their outside patio overlooking a long and ancient stone bridge crossing a dry river bed. I enjoyed a beer (or two) and *tapas* while Maria continued ahead.

Because of the late start I only walked to Calzadilla de la Cueza. It should have been 17.5 Km but with my little detour, my "long cut," I'm guessing it was a little over twenty.

Back to present day. I'm sitting in a room I've just rented, a room in a boarding house near Seattle where I'm living and working, trying to save as much money as possible, hopefully for another 105 weeks as of the time of this writing. I'm literally counting the weeks until I return to Spain to make my next pilgrimage from the Mediterranean coast in Barcelona to Rome, passing through Montserrat so I will have walked, albeit with a three year span in between, the entire distance from the Mediterranean to the Atlantic across the northern part of my adopted homeland. I freely admit that after a couple of glasses of wine my emotions are a little more pronounced, or might I say, a little more free to express themselves. (I've found writing and guitar practice pair very well with just about any vintage and type of wine.) I'm missing Spain. I'm missing the Camino. But most of all I'm missing the friends I left behind. For one brief, shining, short period of my life I was happy and felt bonded with a small group of people such as I've never felt before.

Beer and Debussy

June 21st

I've been one month on the Camino. I started "sauntering" from Montserrat the morning of May 21st, and it's taken me thirty-one days to get to Sahagún. This day I walked solo for the most part and I caught up with Maria about six or seven kilometers before the end of the day. Beth had stayed behind for a little more foot recuperation and planned to take a bus to Sahagún. The bus was full, but remember what I've said about the Camino providing what you need when you need it: She was offered a ride in a car. Funny how things like that kept happening. We dined on pizza and then the girls went back to the albergue to rest while I stayed in the bar and enjoyed a non-pilsner beer for the first time on the Camino.

A couple of notes:

1. Yes, Maria and Beth are grown women, *mujeres* in Spanish, but I was told in no uncertain terms that I was not to refer to them as *mujeres*. *Chicas* (girls) was just fine with them, thank you, so *chicas*, girls it is.

2. I've lived most of my adult life in the Pacific Northwest of the U.S., where variety in beer is a concept held to be more sacred than the 1st and 2nd amendments to *The Constitution*. In and around Seattle and Portland, the minimally provisioned bar will have on tap at least one IPA, one Stout,

one ESB, one seasonal, two lagers and their accompanying "lites," (the horror!). That's just your basic bar, and just what's on tap. Then there will be another dozen types of beer in bottles, and it's not at all uncommon to find a bar with more than a dozen types of beer on tap and twenty-five or more selections in bottle. Beer is serious business around here.

In contrast, I found the normal bar in Spain to have one beer on tap and occasionally hard cider and Shandy, which is a mix of beer and lemonade (and surprisingly good, in my humble opinion). This was the case in small towns and larger cities that I passed through while walking, and even included Granada where I spent another seven weeks after the Camino where I, of course, had the opportunity to visit a number of bars. If you want variety in beer in Spain, your best chance is to find an Irish bar. There you'll be offered, on tap, at least Guinness Stout, an IPA or ESB, an Irish Red, and the normal Cruz Campo, Alhambra or whichever brand is the local favorite lager on tap. In Spain, I suppose, variety in beer just isn't that important. But when it's 100° outside the beer is cold, even in Irish bars, and that's what counts.

As I walked to Sahagún the land was flat but the wind was strong, making the day's walk tiring. I found that walking a little better than an average of twenty-six kilometers a day normally wasn't physically difficult on any part of my body except my feet. With that said, there were a few days around

153

this time where I wasn't tired from walking, but mentally exhausted from fighting the constant wind.

But the wind was what helped to bring about one of those memorable Camino events.

A little background is in order:

Prior to my selling out for the life of a normal working stiff, I had dreamed of being a musician; I'd majored in music in college, and fully intended to make a life of it in some way. Music had been something very special to me, had given me a reason for being, but the practicality of the world after university pulled me down to Earth and I became just another occupant of a cubicle in Corporate America.

Even though music is something near and dear to me, I had set out on my Camino intending not to use my MP3 player to listen to music as I walked. Rather, I just wanted to listen to whatever sounds occurred around me and inside me. Additionally, as God is famous for His still, small voice, I didn't want to take a chance on missing a word should He choose to say something important to me. However, at about this time in my little saunter across the Iberian Peninsula, after about a month, I decided to allow myself a little music if the spirit so moved.

The particular day I was referring to above and a few others like it, I couldn't hear the music because the noise of the wind in my ears would have overpowered it. But there was another

154

day, somewhere near this point in my journey – I didn't note it in my journal but the memory is as clear as if it had happened yesterday – where I was walking alone early one morning with the sun still low in the East and wheat fields all around me. There was more than a breeze but less than a wind and I was listening to Debussy's *La Mer*, a symphonic tone poem evoking images of the sea.

There were a few moments, moments of magic, of ethereal emotion and other-worldliness that occurred on the Camino. This was one of them. As I walked alone, listening to Debussy's tonal images of the sea, I watched the wind move across the tops of the wheat fields and saw, not wheat, but the ocean, with waves and crests undulating in perfect harmony with the music, as if the score had been created exactly for what I was seeing right then and there, as if I were meant to start the music at just the time I did in order to synchronize the motion picture in front of my eyes with the music in my ears. There was rhythm in the movement of the wheat; it was moving to the music. The wind and the motion of the wheat were perfectly linked to the highs and lows in the music, the irregular pulses, the ebb and flow of consonances and dissonances. The emotion of the music was reflected and amplified through the undulations of the wheat in the wind. I was lifted and carried into another existence for just a few moments while Debussy's music played in my ears and God danced in front of my eyes.

155

Poem

Out of Sahagún, walking by myself yet again, I stopped in El Burgo Ranero, just West of Sahagún for lunch. I suppose something about my back pack and my clothing gave me away as a pilgrim. A stranger gave me a card on which was written this poem. Receiving gifts of every kind had become a daily occurrence. If you want to experience the absolute best that human kind has to offer – kindness, the spirit of giving, of concern for one another, a feeling of unity, oneness, solidarity, a shared spirit – walk the Camino de Santiago. Walk the Camino and just try to give more than you receive. It's like trying to out-give God.

I found out later that this is a well-known poem on the Camino. As I re-read it and try to imagine how someone would react to it who had not traveled the Camino, I imagine it wouldn't have the same impact. At the point on the Camino where it was given to me, it brought tears to my eyes and still does.

> The way of Saint James is dust and mud, sun and rain
> Trod by pilgrims in their thousands for more than a
>   thousand years.
> Pilgrim, whose voice is calling you?
> What hidden force leads you on?
> Not the stars of the Milky Way,
> Nor the lure of great cathedrals. It's not the wild heart
>   of Navarre,
> Nor the rich Riojan wines,

Nor the shellfish of Galicia,
Nor the broad Castilian fields. Pilgrim, whose voice
    is calling you?
What hidden force leads you on?
Not the people on your way,
Nor the customs of the land. Not the history or the
    culture,
Not the Cock of La Calzada
Nor the palace of Gaudi,
Nor the castle of Ponferrada. All this I see with
    pleasure,
And, having seen, pass by.
But for me the voice that calls
Comes, I feel, from deep inside. The force that drives
    me on
I can never explain or show.
The force that draws me to it
Only the One above can know.

Eugene Garibay (translated by John Lyon)

El Burgo Ranero to Villandongos del Páramo

June 22nd to 24th

Walking through Mansilla de los Mulas, I stopped at a church to contemplate and rest; not sure which was my main intent. I had considered stopping in León for an extra day of rest, but once I got there, with the crowds and busy streets and another grand cathedral (YAC, Yet Another Cathedral, as I noted in my journal), I just wasn't in the mood. I had been thinking that a day of rest for my worn out feet would be good, but by the time I got there, I decided that the tiredness and soreness were just a fact of life and I knew that resting another day wasn't going to make them any better. They were what they were – flat, misshapen, not really up to the task which I was demanding of them.

If the Camino was a microcosm of my life, then I was represented by my feet. Like them, I wasn't really cut out for what I was doing. I was ill-prepared for the journey and didn't really know where I was going, what each day would bring. The walking, like life itself, was at times difficult and painful but I had no choice but to go on. By early afternoon of each day my feet would be tired and in pain, but I still had kilometers to go. I just put my head down and took another step, then another, then another, until I reached someplace where I could rest for the night. The Camino was a bridge to someplace I had never been: I knew what I had left on one side but I had no idea what was on the other. My faith told me to find out, and that something good would be waiting for me. I had overspent my budget and had given money when I didn't have it to give, but I knew things would turn out OK. Take another step. Right, left, right, left…

I made an entry in my journal on the 23rd in Puente de Villarente while having a Shandy, eating a few slices of *jamón Iberico* (it's not just ham in Spain; you have to know what type of ham), and enjoying the chance to rest. I had just gone to the store with Maria to get something for dinner, but then I realized I had some food left over from the previous day and felt foolish for buying more just when I was beginning to think I ought to watch my money a little more closely. The truth was, I went with her simply because she asked me, without giving it another thought. I hadn't seen Maria all day and missed her so what else was I to do? We were in a small town where there were two grocery stores and a *panadería*, a bread store. But at 6:00 in the evening there was no more bread to be had in town. The people in the stores were so matter-of-fact about it. You want bread? You better get it in the morning when it's fresh and before they sell out. No more until tomorrow. I had never come across a grocery store being out of bread. I'd have to get used to this if a life in Spain was on the other side of the bridge.

I passed through León on the 24th and continued walking after a brief lunch of sardines on the Cathedral steps. It felt good to take my shoes off and just sit in the open air with my can of little fish, watching people, and not having to be concerned about waiters or checks or other restaurant-related preoccupations.

Lunching on sardines on the steps of Cathedral of León, letting my feet breathe. It just doesn't get any better.

I was in the mood for simple. I was also in the mood for some solitude and to get the heck out of Dodge (León), so I got right back up after finishing my lunch, put my boots back on my miserable feet and began walking – in the wrong direction again. *C'est la vie*. I had only gone a few hundred meters when I discovered my error. I felt bad, though, because another pilgrim passed me and asked if I knew if the Camino continued the way we were walking. I told him I thought so. Then when I found out I was wrong, hurriedly tried to catch up to him to inform him that the Camino lay in the opposite direction but he was a fast walker and I couldn't find him. Maybe he ended up in Montserrat. I'll never know.

I finally arrived at the albergue in Valverde de la Virgen to find it closed, shut, out of business. By the weeds growing around the building, it seemed to have been in that state for quite a while. That was at the twenty-four Km mark of that day's walk and the next town was another 8.4 Km away. (I won't mention my feet again in this post, but you know what I'd say if I were to say anything, ¿right?)

Señor perdóname, porque he pecado. (Lord, forgive me, for I have sinned.) I stopped at the next bar on the road to have a cold beer (have I mentioned recently how much I enjoyed drinking as much cold beer as I wanted on the Camino without having to worry about gaining weight?) and to ask if there might, by some remote chance, be another albergue or pension in town. The answer was no, there was not, but sitting at the table next to me was a young couple who said they would be happy to give me a ride in their car to the next town where there was an albergue. Thanking the Camino for giving me exactly what I needed when I needed it, and thanking the couple profusely for the offer of help, I readily accepted and enjoyed a quick, ten-minute drive to the next albergue which

161

would have taken me over two hours with the condition of my feet. (Again, I'm not mentioning what condition they were in – I'm leaving that up to your imagination.) Managing just for this night to give up all pretense of eschewing any transportation other than my own two feet, I arrived at the municipal albergue in Villandangos del Páramo, feeling a little guilty, but managing to deal with those unhelpful emotions with another ice cold beer.

After a long, hot day. El peregrino in Valladongos del Páramo

Back on Track

In an earlier chapter I mentioned that the first couple of decades of my life I thought that music would be my life. I majored in music at the University of Iowa. My instrument was voice. I had dreams of being an opera singer but I learned through five years of voice lessons that I didn't have the volume and sound quality to project over an orchestra. I think I could have trained the larynx and associated musculature to do what they needed to do, but I don't have the nasal "mask," that porous front part of the skull that acts like the sound box of a guitar, violin, or any stringed instrument that gives the resonance we hear as "volume," the quality that makes the sound project over an orchestra. The greatest violinist can have the finest violin strings and bow at his disposal, but if the strings are strung over a cardboard box, Paganini himself couldn't make a decent sound. I was, in effect, trying to sing with a cardboard box as my resonator.

I also saw myself as a choral or orchestral conductor, but that takes a certain personality that I don't seem to have. There is an old joke that goes like this (I'll give you the Reader's Digest version):

> *A great violinist dies and goes to heaven. He finds himself sitting in the Heavenly Orchestra, ready for rehearsal and waiting for the conductor. He's*

somewhat surprised and disoriented but quickly figures out where he is and what's going on. He leans over to the violinist sitting beside him and asks, "Who's the conductor?"

The other violinist replies, "God."

The first violinist says, "Really! How is God as a conductor?"

The other violinist replies, "Well, he's pretty good but, you know, sometimes it seems like he thinks he's Toscanini."

A good conductor has to think, to *believe*, that he's God or Toscanini, take your pick. What's more, he has to convince the rest of the orchestra that he underestimates himself. Think about it: You have a violinist, or a trumpet player, or a cellist, or any instrumentalist in the orchestra who has studied his instrument most of his remembered life, if not longer, and has studied music maybe at a Julliard, or New England School of Music, or Berkeley. They know their stuff. There are fifty, eighty, a hundred of them sitting in front of the conductor and he has to tell them how to do their jobs. He has to tell them that his way of playing the piece is better than their way and get all of them to perform exactly as he wants. And for that to work, they all have to believe that the conductor knows best. The conductor, the great conductor (and why be any other kind?) has to inspire faith among the members of the orchestra that they normally reserve only for God.

By the time a person completes a bachelor's degree, he knows whether he has that personality. Or at least, in my case, it was apparent that I did not have it. (Musical talent? That's hard to say. But let's address one problem at a time.) I admit, not every conductor in the world making a living as such has that personality. But you have to have at least some of that to get started and that's simply not who I am. I remember getting confirmation in the mail that I had completed all the course work for my bachelor of music degree and thinking, as I held the paper in my hands, "Now what do I do?" I was engaged. I was going to be married and have a family and I didn't want to lead a family through what I knew would be a difficult life of no money and no security while I tried to eke out a living as an itinerant adjunct music professor.

So I decided it was time to grow up and I went back to school to get a Master of Business Administration degree, an MBA: the key to financial success. Except I couldn't stand the subject or the coursework, no matter how much I tried to tell myself that I did. I left after three semesters of part-time school.

During those three semesters I had taken a course in computer programming which was just enough to get an interview with Control Data Corp., CDC, in Chicago. They were hiring a few people for a team to travel the state of Indiana for about a year, converting various credit unions' data processing systems from Merchants' Bank of Indiana to that of CDC.

Merchants' was leaving the business of deposit and loan data processing for credit unions and had endorsed CDC as their successor, so there was a lot of work to be done in a short time. That was my entry into technical project management where I've made my career ever since.

Moving forward just a few years after the start of my technical project management career, I began having a recurring dream that was to continue with me until June 25th, 2012. There were actually two dreams, but both meant the same thing:

In the first, I have to take a university final exam for a class that I forgot I had registered for, or that, for some reason, I had never attended. Whatever the reason, I had to take a test in some subject I was not prepared for and about which I knew absolutely nothing.

In the second dream, *it's opening night for a play or a musical for which I have never rehearsed. Again, either I forgot or didn't know that I was in the play. But here I am, opening night, due to go on stage in a few minutes and I have no idea what my lines or my songs are.*

I haven't studied the psychological and dream theories of Carl Jung, but I can interpret those dreams pretty easily: I'm someplace where I don't belong. Those weren't dreams of an anxious college student before final exams; they were about my career. They were telling me that I'm a fish out of water, unprepared, going the wrong direction. In the dream, the exams for which I was sitting were for subjects I have no interest in, typically math or science-related. What am I doing taking math and science courses? My heart's not in those areas. As far as the other dream goes, I might like to be in a play or musical, but I left that life behind and haven't done anything in that area for decades. I didn't have those dreams once or twice; I had them countless times over the course of twenty-eight years. They played over and over in my sleep like a number one song on a pop radio station.

It didn't take very many years into my technical project management career, maybe five or six, to figure out what those dreams were telling me: I had made a turn in my life that took me off the path I had planned for myself before I was born. (That's my belief, take it or leave it.) But what could I do? I had responsibilities and felt trapped. Six years into the career world, I returned to school in order to complete my MBA so that I could at least advance to a better job. Before I registered for classes I almost changed to the MA in Music Theory and History program but I chickened out, finished my MBA in 1990, and have been a technical project manager ever since.

Walking the Camino in Spain, having planned to leave the world of project management and corporate America, I felt good – better than good, and it was an everyday, morning to night feeling. I was relaxed, purposeful, happy: no Prozac required. I had decided to remain in Spain and find work as an English teacher. I've volunteered as an English teacher for immigrants here in the U.S., had taken language teaching courses, receiving a certificate in teaching English as a Foreign Language a couple of years ago. I enjoyed teaching, was fulfilled by it. Later, in Granada, I met people associated with the university there and discussed various topics in music history with them and got names of professors to follow up with to begin my own private study of music history, specifically the music of Spain. I spoke with the director of the choir of the Granada Cathedral about being part of the choir (I don't have an opera voice, but no chorus has ever turned me away.) Things were falling into place and I could see that I was getting my life back on track in my adopted homeland.

June 26th

I woke up in the middle of the night after a different dream, one that I remembered in detail. *I was in a classroom taking a final exam, but this time the exam was in music theory 101. I was confident. I knew my stuff. The dream continued to where I received my score on the exam – 100 percent! The professor couldn't believe that anyone could do that well; no one in any of her classes had ever managed to get that score.* Back in my undergraduate days I received a 4.0 average in music theory classes. As an entering freshman I took CLEP exams (College Level Examination Program) to pass out of my university core courses and tested out of all of them except one science and one speech class. By so doing I had time to take extra music classes and by the time I graduated with my bachelor's degree I had taken several graduate-level music theory and analysis classes, receiving A's in all of them. I only say that to indicate that if I have a talent, that's where it is. In my dream I was in my element, back home where I was supposed to be. In the dream I was in a basic music theory class which I interpreted to mean I was back on track, but that I had wasted a lot of time and lost a lot of ground for which I'm now going to have to compensate. I'll have to back up, retrace my steps, go back to Theory 101 and re-learn things that I've forgotten.

But the important thing is that I was back on track with my life's plan. I hadn't felt so good in decades.

Foncebedon and The Cruz de Fierro

June 25th (continued):

The night of the dream noted in the previous chapter I slept the entire night. This was unusual – unusual on the Camino as well as in "real life." On the Camino I'd normally be awakened by the sound of snoring or, in "the real world," just because my body told me to wake up for some inexplicable reason in the wee hours of the morning. Nothing unusual, that, but walking across Spain I would ask myself why, after walking twenty-five, thirty, or thirty-five kilometers and being completely exhausted, could I not sleep through the night? But this night, June 25th, I slept and it seemed that I dreamed the entire night.

Indulge me. I have no idea what this these dreams might mean, but I remembered them so vividly that they've become part of my Camino experience. Maybe someday I'll figure them out, or go to a Jungian analyst and get some help.

After the dream of the music test,

> *I dreamed of a girl who had a pain in her left hip.* (Maria was experiencing a problem with her left hip; it bothered her much of the time while she walked.) *In my dream another girl had a natural, herbal cure for the suffering girl's (Maria's?) hip, requiring that I place an herbal poultice, over the course of several*

treatments, directly into the hip socket. For the final treatment, the "healer," provider of the poultice, summoned a crow that would bring the herbs in its beak, but what the crow was bringing for this treatment was something different: It was not the cure, but an herb that, once placed in the ailing girl's hip joint would kill her. Somehow, the plot was discovered and the girl avoided having the deadly herbs placed in her hip joint, but the "healer," the girl who summoned the crow to bring the herbs, began shooting at me with a six-shot revolver. She fired five shots at me and missed each time. Running, I entered a room where there happened to be another person whom I didn't know. I shut the door and waited for the sixth shot.

There the dream ended. I have no idea what it meant, but because it was so vivid and because I remembered it so well, I noted it in my journal and relate it here. Maybe someone who is reading this has an interpretation. Send me an email.

I then had another dream directly after that one.

Two wolves had come out of nearby woods and were endangering my mother's house and property. I was in a horse-drawn carriage explaining to my passenger, a life-long friend (who recommended Elizabeth Gilbert's Eat, Pray, Love, *mentioned in an earlier chapter), that these wolves were a danger to my mother and I had to deal with them. I pointed out to her that these were not "mere" coyotes, but were dangerous gray wolves. They made no threatening moves during the dream, but I knew they would be a problem in the future and I had to do something about them, and the sooner the better.*

So much for my dreams.

Qué día, "What a day!" I noted in my journal again at the end of that day. Maria and I had been walking with some other pilgrims whom we had seen off and on for the last couple of weeks. We walked the last four kilometers, more or less, uphill, and were all very tired. We stayed at the albergue *Monte Irago* in Foncebedon. We had passed up the previous pueblo and albergue, choosing instead to walk the extra few kilometers to get to Foncebedon because my guide book said there was a very unusual and wonderful restaurant, the most unique on the Camino, in this pueblo. My guide book was correct. The ambiance was indescribable – Celtic music, eclectic, old world décor, with a stone mosaic of a goose in the middle of the floor. I had a wonderful dinner of venison, so tender and delicious it must have been in a marinade for three days. Celtic music, candles, wonderful food, Maria: I was in heaven.

This pueblo, Foncebedon, had been abandoned for a century or more but had in the last decade or so, been resuscitated due to the pilgrim traffic. There was not one, but two albergues, each offering a full dinner, in addition to the restaurant referred to above. From the outside, it still looked like a ghost town, but the twenty-five residents of the pueblo had created an extremely comfortable and inviting rest stop on the Camino.

Entering Foncebedon

The next day Maria and I reached the Cruz de Fierro, the Cross of Iron. This is a significant stop along the Camino, a place of rich tradition where pilgrims leave a stone that they have carried at the foot of the cross and say a prayer for their own blessing, or for the blessing of another. I had carried, for people I loved, several stones across Spain in a small pocket in my back pack, intending to leave them with prayers at the foot of the Cruz de Fierro.

I didn't take any pictures here; the experience was too powerful, the place too holy. To take pictures would have desecrated the cross and the experience.

Thinking about places and experiences too powerful to desecrate with a camera, I'm reminded of a group of people I crossed paths with in this region: three people on foot and their companion in a wheel chair. The wheel chair was rigged with a harnesses that allowed two people to pull while the third pushed. I couldn't bring myself to photograph them. As I wrote *"Que día"* in my journal, my difficult day of climbing hills, I thought of these people who pushed and pulled their friend along the Camino: a challenging walk for one person in good shape, but ten times more difficult for those pushing and pulling their wheel chair-bound friend through the Pyrenees, across the *llanura*, through rain and wind, up and down the hills of Galicia, and more. The Bible says, "There is no greater love than to lay down one's life for one's friends."

No, but those who push and pull their friend in a wheel chair on the Camino de Santiago are a close second.

It's difficult to imagine the emotional impact of the *Cruz*, of the hardship of the walking, the blisters, the feet screaming in pain by the end of each day. Just as it's difficult, if not impossible, to imagine the sense of peace as one experiences solitude, simplicity, and silence of the Camino, to experience the instant friendship, camaraderie, and sometimes even love of other pilgrims one meets along the way. Some experiences, some feelings, can't be described. John Steinbeck himself couldn't begin to convey the emotions that surround a spiritual pilgrim at the *Cruz de Fierro*, much less what surrounds one throughout the entire hundreds of kilometers of the Camino. After completing three-fourths of the path and experiencing feelings I never could have imagined, when I finally arrived at this point, I admit that I wept once more at the foot of the cross, saying prayers for those I love and for whom I carried stones across Spain.

As I removed the stones representing family and friends from the pocket in my back pack and sat under the eve of the small chapel near the cross, rain falling silently, I said *The Pilgrim's Prayer* for each person, with their stone in my hand, picturing in my mind's eye the person for whom I was praying. I tailored the prayer to meet each person's circumstances. Not all of us make a pilgrimage to the city of Santiago, but we are all, each of us, on our own pilgrimage to our own Santiago:

> *Lord, you who recalled your servant Abraham out of the town Ur in Chaldea and who watched over him during all his wanderings; You who guided the Jewish people through the desert; we also query to watch your present servants, who for love for Your name, make a pilgrimage to Santiago de Compostela, Be for us:*

175

A companion on our journey,
The guide on our intersections,
The strengthening during fatigue,
The fortress in danger,
The resource on our itinerary,
The shadow in our heat,
The light in our darkness,
The consolation during dejection,
And the power of our intention,
So that we under your guidance, safely and unhurt,
may reach the end of our journey and strengthened
with gratitude and power, secure and filled with
happiness, may join our home.
For Jesus Christ, Our Lord. Amen. Apostle James,
pray for us.
Holy Virgin, Pray for us.

Manjarín and Ponferrada

June 27th

I didn't make an entry in my journal for the next week. It was at about this point, where I calculated I was about two weeks from the end of the Camino, that I began feeling the abyss: the end of the Camino. I knew I should just be enjoying each moment, but I'm a "futures" kind of guy – I'm always and forever thinking about what's coming. From my vantage point here on the Camino, I had no idea what the future would bring and, while I was planning to remain in Spain and was looking forward to it, still, the idea of the end of the Camino was depressing to say the least. I was enjoying every day and feeling more attached to Maria each minute, but I knew all this was coming to an end and I began feeling the same lump in the pit of my stomach as I had each Sunday night when I was back in the real world, thinking about the coming week of work and stress. I was still having wonderful experiences and felt I was walking at the edge of heaven, but everything comes to an end and the horizon was now not so far away.

For whatever reason, I stopped writing in my journal for about a week so I'll have to rely on my memory, a few photographs I took, and small notes in my guidebook for a while.

From the *Cruz de Fierro*, the next "pueblo" you pass through is Manjarín, which must be the smallest pueblo in Spain. It comprises one house which is the dwelling of what is reputed to be the last Knight Templar. My guide book informs me that this was a camp and rest stop for Roman troops. It says there are few comforts here, but much *ambiente templario*, (Templar ambiance) and is a place the pilgrim may or may not like, but will leave with a definite impression of some kind.

The entire pueblo of Manjarin

They were right, and my impression was haunting and mystical, even amidst the tables of trinkets and souvenirs for sale. The medieval music playing barely audibly through hidden speakers added a magical touch. There was a sense of great age and wisdom in the small shelter. How that's possible in an old building I don't know, but it was there, as well as a sense of welcoming and relaxation. It would have been perfect to just spend a few years there, but we had to move on.

On June 27th we arrived in Ponferrada, a city that owes its existence to the Romans and nearby gold mines. Much later, in 1082, the local bishop ordered an old wooden bridge over the River *Sil* replaced with one of iron, bringing more commerce to the city. Then, about a hundred years later a fortress was built and occupied by nuns to protect pilgrims on their way to Santiago de Compostela.

The fortress at Ponferrada

It was about this time, if memory serves, that I discovered *Pulpo de Galicia* – octopus prepared in the Galician style. (Yes, even though we were still in León and had quite a ways to go before reaching Galicia proper.) I've never been much of a fan of cephalopods as a food, but I'll make an exception when it's cooked in the Galician style. I don't know what they do to it or how it's prepared, other than using the obvious sweet paprika and olive oil, but it was heavenly. Maybe it was a combination of the ambiance of Northwest Spain: cool weather, rolling, green hills dotted by ancient pueblos, the hint of a Gaelic heritage, complete with bagpipes. I rarely passed up an opportunity to sample the local *pulpo* at each bar I stopped at. It became my favorite *tapa*.

As I walked through this beautiful, lush region of Spain, and as I think back with help from the photos I took, I felt, and can still feel, an attachment to the country that I've never been able to muster for anyplace I've lived in the United States. When I was a child, my family moved frequently, owing to my father's career, so I never had the opportunity to develop feelings of home for a location, a part of the country or a city. Even when I got older and my family stopped moving so much, I didn't feel any attachment to a city, a state, or even the country in which I lived. I chalked this up to having lived the gypsy lifestyle, never settling in one place during those early years of life when we develop attachments to the land, a region, or a culture. Feeling an attachment to a geographical region was not even in my capacity to imagine in the past. But here, in León and later in Galicia, it was obvious and easy to comprehend how people could feel oneness with their pueblo and with their region of Spain, how one could feel that, absent their homeland, they would be incomplete.

I had never had that feeling, but nevertheless I missed it and envied Gallegos and all Spaniards for having it.

A slate hanging on a tree. Signs of encouragement are common on the Camino

Lord, Grant Me Patience

In Ponferrada we found a grand, as in *muy grande*, albergue converted from an old cathedral. An upper floor had been created where there were now at least 200 beds, arranged as bunk beds in cubicles of eight beds in each, if memory serves. It was a way of turning a cavernous bunkhouse into a fairly pleasant arrangement with some small sense of privacy, if such a thing is possible in a bunkhouse of over two-hundred beds. There was also a very well-equipped kitchen and dining area.

As a side note, I think if I wanted to walk the Camino again, and wanted and could select my travel partner, I'd walk with an Asian or group of Asians; they eat better than anyone on the Camino. Dinners and even breakfasts were full out, multi-course meals. For the most part, everyone else, myself included, tended to go for simplicity, calories, and carbohydrates. The Asians, on the other hand, if I might be allowed to generalize a little, tended to prepare full, healthy, colorful, delicious meals, complete with rice, pot stickers, sautéed vegetables, meats, and just about anything and everything imaginable. It was amazing to behold what they could prepare given the limited cooking facilities in the albergues. I have to admit, though, that it was only my laziness that kept me from having better meals at most albergues along the way. Fresh fruits and vegetables were common in just about any pueblo I passed through, and most albergues had rudimentary cooking equipment and a small, but serviceable kitchen that would allow meal preparation if one were so inclined.

I believe it was here, in Ponferrada, where I finally bought another pair of sunglasses. Maria and I went walking around the town looking for a grocery store, which we easily found, and bought something easy to prepare for dinner and some cherries. I only mention the cherries because I learned what the number "4" means. Remember, I said I enjoyed studying languages and here's one of the reasons. We were at a fruit stand and Maria asked for four cherries. Yes, four (4) cherries. The clerk casually put in a handful of cherries in the bag. Maria, didn't seem to think that that was quite enough, so asked for four (4) more. The clerk put another, albeit smaller, handful in the bag. Maria took the bag of cherries and we proceeded to check out. I must have had a confused look on my face, or, more confused than normal, and Maria explained to me that "four" in this case doesn't mean four, but several, a handful. If that's not quite enough and you ask for four more, it's understood that you want a few more, but not as many as in the first go-round. Four, as in more than three and less than five has nothing to do with the transaction.

I had been looking for someplace to buy another pair of sunglasses to replace the ones I had left behind but had been unsuccessful. It's not as easy as you might think, if you're an

American, where you can find a cheap pair of sunglasses in any drug or grocery store, or just about any type of store for that matter. In Spain, that's not the way it is. You might find a general, or variety store in a large city, normally run by Asian immigrants, that carry all manner of things, but in the small towns you walk through on the Camino you find grocery stores, which carry groceries, drug stores, which carry over-the-counter and prescription medications, or a hardware store, which, of course carries hardware, etc. If you want to buy sunglasses, you have to go to a store that sells glasses. Luckily, or not, depending on your interpretation of the story, we found an eye glass store. We walked in and I began trying on sunglasses. The clerk was very helpful, as was Maria, helping me to find just the right pair for the shape of my face and that even accentuated the "salt and pepper" coloring of my hair at the temples. (Yes, that's really true.) After twenty minutes of trying on glasses and narrowing down the selection to the perfect pair, I said I'd take them and whipped out the credit card. It wasn't until then that I asked how much they were. I think in another life I might try to make a career playing poker because I believe (and from the lack of reaction on the part of the clerk and Maria to my reaction, that belief is well placed) that I must have kept a perfect poker face when I heard the amount. Sure, no problem. Put it on the card. I am, after all, an American movie stare in disguise. Money is no object. As long as the glasses accentuate and compliment my suddenly grayer hair.

I've said it before, but I'll say it again, "Marge, sometimes I'm just not too bright." I just couldn't stand the thought of the embarrassment that would ensue were I to say, after all that time, "I can't afford that!" I know, it's silly, but that's the way I am. Someday I'll learn to ask about the price before I find the perfect glasses or shoes or whatever it is I'm buying. I had already felt foolish a number of times in front of Maria with my lack of Spanish, thinking I understood something and finding out later I completely missed the mark, or saying or doing the wrong thing. This time I was just going to have to suck it up and pay three times more for a pair of sunglasses than I had planned. What the heck. It's only money.

Well, anyway, I have a nice, *very nice* pair of sunglasses as a memento of my evening spent in Ponferrada.

Who is that movie star behind those expensive Ray Ban glasses
that so delicately accentuate his salt-and-pepper temples?

From Ponferrada we walked through Colombrianos, Fuentes
Nuevas, Companaraya, Cacabelos, and reached Villafranca
del Bierzo on June 28th The weather had gone from hundred-
degree days in the sun in Catalunya and Aragón to cool and
cloudy during the day here in the northwest part of Spain, and
was down-right chilly in the mornings. The sunglasses stayed
in their case most of the time and I had to buy a long-sleeve
shirt to wear over a t-shirt to stay warm during the morning
hours. We had a couple of days of rain during this stage of
the Camino, but I felt fortunate that that's all we had. I'd heard

of other pilgrims walking through weeks of rain, so I was grateful for this.

The next day, June 29th, we walked through Pereje, Trabadelo, La Portela, Ambasmestas, Vega de Valcarce, Ruitelan, Las Herrerías, La Faba, Laguna de Castilla, and finally stopped at O Cebreiro for the night. All these pueblos we passed through in less than twenty-eight kilometers. People I talk with about having walked the Camino, who have no idea of what it is, ask if I had to camp out and wonder if I had to carry a lot of food with me. The simple answer is no, and in fact the challenge in this part of the Camino, as opposed to many days in Catalunya and Aragón, is that there are too many bars to stop at, too many opportunities for rest. Sometimes it's difficult to not stop at every pueblo for beer and tapas. In all the pueblos listed above except La Faba and Laguna de Castilla there were ample opportunities for food and drink.

The country here is beautiful - lush, green, bucolic, dotted with hills, each populated with, horses, cattle, and sheep. We also found, much to my surprise, forests of eucalyptus trees. The sense of smell was constantly bombarded by the polar opposites of eucalyptus and manure used for fertilizer at every farm.

I have an affinity for Andalucía. I don't know why, but flamenco dance and music and the Muslim and Mudehar architecture has a lot to do with it. However, I have to admit, walking through León I started to wonder if I might want to settle in this area of Spain. There is a word that is used to describe flamenco dancers–*duende*–which literally means "ghost" because the word is derived from the phrase *dueño de la casa*, owner of the house, and refers to the ghost of a previous owner who has remained after death to haunt the house. (This according to *Nuevas fascinantes historias de las palabras* by Ricardo Soca.) It has come to mean "spirit" in the sense of that which inhabits the best and most gifted flamenco dancers who express their own *duende* through their dance. But there is also a *duende* in Galicia and it's real and strong and palpable in every pueblo you pass through and even in the air as you walk through the country. When I remember and think about this part of the Camino I feel very introspective and emotional. It's not something I can talk about even a year after the experience. The entire Camino evokes the same feeling, but it's stronger here. Maybe it's because I knew that I was approaching the end of the best fifty days of my life. Maybe it was the experience of the *Cruz de Fierro* which drove a stake through the heart of any vestiges of my previous life that remained after the previous experiences of the Camino. Or maybe it's because there really was a *duende* here in every sense of the word that began to haunt me. Probably, as with all things in life, it was a combination of all these, and more that deny enumeration.

The attraction of Spain, of the Camino, of León and Galicia is so strong as I write and think about my experiences there that I am on the very cusp of simply leaving for Spain on the next flight, ignoring all my financial and personal responsibilities which brought me back to the States last September. It's only a well-developed sense of responsibility and guilt that keeps me from pitching everything at this very moment and returning to Spain immediately. If God will allow me the patience, I'll stay here until I can return debt-free and maybe even with a little money in the bank to make a new life in my adopted homeland.

Leaving O Cebreiro, just over the border into Galicia from León

Leaving O Cebreiro

June 30th

Leaving O Cebreiro it seemed every kilometer was more beautiful than the last. At this altitude, between 4,000 and 5,000 feet, the clouds seem to hang just above your head, slightly out of reach, covering the tops of the lush, green hills that surround you. Every pueblo seems to be carved out of the earth. The stonework is masterful; houses and barns seem to be integral parts of the landscape. We normally walked far from any roads that might carry traffic so we were enveloped in silence broken only by lowing of cows and the bleating of sheep off in the distance, or sometimes sharing the Camino with us as they were moved from pasture to pasture. It rained much of the day between O Cebreiro and Triacastela, but it was only heavy for the first five and a half kilometers. I had a rain coat which kept my upper body dry but my pants were soaked. As I mentioned before, I didn't care for the synthetic shirts I had bought for the trip, but the pants, specifically designed to be light and easy to care for, were comfortable and dried fast. I was glad not to be wearing cotton jeans. For any future pilgrims who might be reading this I'd also recommend the style of pants with zip-off legs so they can be converted into shorts without having to undress to change clothes mid-day. With the cool mornings turning into warm afternoons, the convenience of convertibility often came in handy.

From Villafranca to O Cebreiro the route climbs about 700 meters (not feet, meters!) over ten kilometers and makes for a good day's hike. O Cebreiro and a comfortable albergue is a welcome sight for sore legs. The next day we descended about the same altitude over ten kilometers which would normally be a welcome relief, but there was one long section with a steep downgrade that was a workout, to say the least, for fifty-five-year-old knees, one of which had been damaged thirty-five years earlier while training for a week's hike in the Grand Canyon. To add insult to injury, my feet, as I think I've mentioned, were not designed for extended walking in the first place and by now were permanently swollen. I wouldn't have believed it was possible, but they had even swollen lengthwise so my normally crowded toes were feeling very unwelcome in the front of my boots. The long downhill walk was worse than going uphill, my toes jammed against the front of my boots. I never felt more relieved than when I arrived at flat terrain when we reached Triacastela.

For most of the day I walked alone. Sometimes I'd catch up with Maria at rest stops. I missed her company but she wanted and needed some solitude. Going back through this, re-reading, proofing, thinking about the Camino, it may seem like Maria and I had a fairly one-sided relationship; she's always wanting solitude and I'm always trying to catch up with her. But I'm intentionally leaving out narrative of the times we spent together out of respect for her privacy and to avoid guessing how I think she felt. Maria told me many times that she didn't want a relationship with anyone, at least not now. But there were just as many times over the weeks where I wasn't sure that she was completely sure about that. In the end, (spoiler alert!) the "no relationship" side won. But for several brief, shining weeks over the course of the Camino, I felt an extreme closeness to her and today can't even begin to imagine how I would have experienced the Camino without Maria's presence.

I didn't mind walking alone, but as I had grown somewhat, or more than somewhat attached to Maria, I had mixed feelings about my own solitude at this point on the Camino.

My thoughts alternated between, "Wouldn't it be nice if I could spend some time after the Camino with this woman, as in, oh, about a lifetime or so…" and, "Stop being a foolish old man." (Maria is twenty years younger than I.) As I found myself thinking the former more and more, my actions and words tended to reflect the latter. I'd make a fool of myself and end up hurting Maria's feelings, then I'd feel like more of a fool and get frustrated by my inability to communicate, both because my Spanish was inadequate and because my dueling emotions tended to result in a behavior that reflected just about anything other than what I was really feeling.

So we, or I, walked on through Liñares, Hospital, Alto do Poio, Fonfría, and O Viduedo, stopping at Triacastela for the night. The following day was a short 18.5 Km walk to Sarria where I stopped for the night for a farewell dinner with a fellow pilgrim and Maria continued on to avoid the crowds that gather in this pueblo to begin their Camino, as it's the shortest walk to Santiago that still allows one to claim their Compostela – their "certificate of achievement." We said *hasta luego*, see you later, and talked about meeting up somewhere along the way, but I had a sinking feeling I'd never see her again.

Sarria

July 1st

The Camino giveth and the Camino taketh away. We said *buen camino* to each other and as easily as if we'd just met in passing, Maria turned and walked down the road. I guess she didn't care for long goodbyes. I watched her walk away until she was out of sight and then watched a little longer, wondering if she'd fulfill my fantasy of suddenly reappearing, walking back to me, as if this were a movie; Tom Hanks could play my part, Meg Ryan hers.

She didn't come back.

Maybe there will be a sequel.

I stayed in Sarria to have a farewell dinner with James, a fellow pilgrim I had met along the way a couple of weeks prior. He was from England and had started the Camino the previous year at this point. This year, he started in St Jean Pied de Port and walked to Sarria in order to complete the entire traditional French route of the Camino. I met a few pilgrims along the way who were taking two, three, or even four years to walk the Camino in stages. They only had limited time away from work, so walked as far as they could one year, returning to start where they left off as many times as required to complete their Camino. (Let me just say once and leave it at that: Work can really get in the way of life.) In the same vein, I've decided to begin my next pilgrimage to Rome at the Mediterranean shore in Barcelona and make my route through Monistrol, the gateway to Montserrat, which is a bit out of the way, but by doing so I will have walked the entire breadth of Spain from the Mediterranean to the Atlantic. Not that that's important from any pilgrimage perspective; it just seems a cool thing to do.

In Sarria I checked into a pension, which was more expensive than one of the several albergues but I was feeling the need to have a little solitude myself here, and was looking forward to a night without snoring and the requisite ear plugs. At dinner time, 8:00 or so, I went to the restaurant where James' friends were giving him his going away dinner and found a seat at a long table, sitting across from Tilly, a woman from Leipzig whom I'd met a few days earlier, a sometime walking companion of James. She was with a couple of other women from Germany, Katalyn and another whose name I didn't write down and is lost forever in my faulty memory. As the dinner wound down and the others left the table, I remained to talk with Tilly whom I found to be another fascinating, warm, and engaging person. The truth is, there are no "non-fascinating, non-warm, and non-engaging" people on the Camino. Take some time to get to know just a little about whomever you meet and you'll find a new friend. Leipzig was in the former East Germany and Tilly was just old enough to remember the time before the fall of the Wall. I've mentioned before that in my previous life I was a wannabe musician (OK, I still am) and was so jealous to learn that Tilly had sung in a children's choir under Kurt Masur in one of the greatest cities of music in the world. She had just completed university and would start her career after the Camino as a French and biology high school teacher.

Tilly and I talked about many things and I mentioned that I was interested in the question of why there was no well-known tradition of music from Spain, other than flamenco and what has come to be known as "Spanish" guitar, or the classical guitar tradition.

(Parenthetical thought, if you don't mind me interrupting myself. I was talking with Tilly in English. She was a well-educated German, so of course spoke her native language perfectly. She also spoke French well enough to teach it at the German high school level, which is much more rigorous than what is normally taught in a U.S. high school, and was able to get along quite well in Spain speaking their language. I was reminded of a joke: *What do you call a person who speaks three languages? Trilingual. What do you call a person who speaks two languages? Bilingual. What do you call a person who speaks one language? American.* Ha-ha. Not really funny, is it?)

Anyway, getting back to the music of Spain. Spain has its *Zarzuelas*, which might be most comparable to *opéra comique* or comic light opera, and, yes, there are several

Spanish composers whose music is part of the standard orchestral repertoire: Manuel de Falla, Juaquín Turina, Isaac Albéniz among some of the best known. But if the number of composers and their works from the other European countries were weighed against those of Spain, the Spanish repertoire of commonly performed orchestral, and especially choral music, would be very light indeed. After the Camino, spending several weeks in Granada, I also spoke with a history professor from the University of Granada who, not surprisingly, took some offense at my proposition that the musical tradition of Spain, at least in its quantity, lagged behind that of some other European countries. His thesis was that the apparent dearth of music was only that: apparent. The truth, in his opinion, was that there was a long and vibrant tradition of "classical" music from Spain but that for some reason it had not been promoted to the extent of music from Germany, France, Italy, etc. Further study of the question while in Granada seemed to confirm at least some truth to his thesis, but then that begged the question: Why was the music of Spain not promoted throughout the world as had been the music of the rest of Europe? Still, I don't believe, at least at this point in my study of the question, that lack of promotion is the entire explanation for the comparatively small canon of orchestral, operatic, and choral music from Spain.

Getting back to my new friend, Tilly, she suggested that possibly the answer had something to do with the patronage, or rather, the lack of royal and ecclesiastical patronage of composers and performers compared with their counterparts in the rest of Europe. The instrumental musical tradition of Europe owes much of its existence to kings and the Catholic and protestant churches. For example, a large portion of the choral and instrumental opus of Bach is due to the patronage of Leopold, Prince of Anhalt-Koethen for whom Bach was *kapellmeister* and to August III as his court composer. Handel wrote much of his music as the court composer for King George II of England.

I don't know if the question of patronage has a correlation with the amount of orchestral and choral music of Spain, but it was an interesting discussion and kindled memories of my earlier life as a wannabe musician and I completed the evening feeling, still and again, that I was back on track. (And I'll have to admit I was thoroughly enjoying Tilly's company, not only for the stimulating conversation about music, but because she was very intelligent and a good conversationalist. I wish I could have gotten to know her better.)

As a final note on the subject, only a few months ago I was browsing the internet, looking for information on the general subject of Spanish music, and found a reference to a doctoral thesis by a student at a Spanish university on the very topic of lack of patronage of Spanish musicians and composers. I think Tilly had a good idea. I'll continue to look into it.

I almost expected to see flying monkeys and the wicked witch
flying through the air as we walked through this forest.

Gonzar

July 2nd

After a good night's sleep sans snoring (at least, none but my own, which I couldn't hear), I left Sarria amidst a veritable throng of humanity. I noted in my journal that, compared with the Camino prior to arriving at this waypoint, it now seemed as if I were walking in Grand Central Station. Sarria is the traditional starting point for those who want, for whatever reason (no judgment here) to walk the minimum distance, one hundred kilometers, in order to be registered as a pilgrim in the annals of the Camino de Santiago. I noted the much smaller back packs and casual clothing of the "day-trippers," as I referred to them (without judgment, of course).

99.5 kilometers to Santiago

It was here that I started taking notice if the stone markers indicating the kilometers to Santiago with mixed emotions. (Mixed emotions seemed to be the theme of my life.) First,

Only 99.5 Km to go to Santiago! Then, Shit! Only 99.5 Km to go to the end of my walk along the outskirts of heaven.

I walked from Sarria through Barbadelo, Rente, Brea, Ferreiros, Mercadoiro, Vilachá, and finally reached Portomarín, a large town with six albergues and three hostels. Each of which I avoided. Because most pilgrims were following a popular guidebook, the same one I had, they would stop for the night at the suggested waypoint of Portomarín. This would have been a respectable 22.4 Km for the day; not a great distance, and certainly not so great that I couldn't walk another eight kilometers to Gonzar, about an hour and forty-five minutes at my end-of-day pace, and well worth the effort in order to put some distance between the crowds and myself.

I took a brief rest for a beer and tapas and mailed some post cards, then continued on my way. The walk continued to be beautiful – every turn around the bend brought scenery more and more captivating; lush, with the smells of eucalyptus, alternating warmth of the sun in open areas and cool air in the forests. The weather was perfect and the truth is, I wanted to relish every painful step, knowing that my Camino was coming to an end. Another couple of hours to Gonzar didn't bother me at all.

I checked into the municipal albergue, the first one I came to, and found no comfortable area to relax as was common in most albergues. There was only a tiny, ill-equipped kitchen and no dining area. The only common area was behind the albergue where people were washing clothing in an outdoor laundry sink. There were only a few outdoor chairs available; all of them taken. After claiming a bunk with my back pack, I took my journal and a pen and set out to find a bar where I could get a glass of wine (or two) and make some notes. (OK, maybe three glasses.) What I found was another albergue; this one with a restaurant and respectable bar, very friendly staff, a lounge area, a good selection of *Rioja vino tinto*, and, wait for it, Tilly and the other German girls! Life was good again. I quickly registered and returned to the municipal albergue to retrieve my back pack. I didn't immediately see the *hospitalera* and figured that no one had ever made a bed-check in other albergues, why should this one be any different? There didn't seem to be any shortage of beds, so forgive me, but I just left without telling anyone. I hoped that no one who could have had a bed was turned away at the end of the day because of my malfeasance. The municipal albergue had cost five Euros, the private, ten, so I ended up paying fifteen Euros for the night. But, being tired and hungry, and looking forward to a comfortable night, a good meal, and very pleasant companionship – I really didn't care.

I had a nice dinner with Tilly and Katalyn, sharing a couple of bottles of wine (they had one, I had the other). They and a couple of other pilgrims who had been walking with them for most of the Camino became my walking companions from here to Santiago.

I had become resolved to my fate that my Camino would end in just a few days, but Tilly suggested that I continue walking on to Finisterre, which, along with Muxia if one chooses, is the real end of the Santiago de Compostela pilgrimage, regardless of the name.

I was told by one *hospitalero* that the symbol of the pilgrimage to Santiago that pilgrims attach to their back packs, the scallop shell, is actually not to be received and carried until one gets to the end of the Camino at Finisterre or Muxia. In centuries past it was a symbol that the pilgrim had actually made the pilgrimage all the way to the ocean. In those days there were no buses or airplanes for the return trip. The pilgrim would collect a scallop shell from the shore and carry it home, walking of course, as a symbol of having completed the pilgrimage the entire way to the Atlantic Ocean.

I had thought, especially as I limped into Lleída some weeks prior, that I wouldn't take another step past Santiago. A bus to the coast seemed, back then, to be a darned good idea. Now it was different. I was no more ready for the end of the Camino than a condemned man is for his last meal. Convincing me to continue on, walking the extra 80 Km to the Atlantic coast was an easy argument for Tilly to make. I breathed a sigh of relief – I had a stay of execution for four more days of Camino bliss.

One Miracle After Another...

July 2nd

I had gone through the first stage of the Camino alone, then enjoyed companionship of Maria, Beth, and, at least for part of the time, with Annick for the second stage which ended at Sarria, and now was walking in an on-again/off-again partnership with Tilly and the other German girls during the final days to Santiago. This particular day was one of the "off-again" days and I found myself walking mostly alone through the farmland of Galicia. All along the Camino I had been listening for the voice of God, for instruction, inspiration, guidance, anything. I know, or at least I believe, that God and His angels are always talking to us but we're normally deaf to their voices and blind to their subtle signals. Well, I can't really speak for others, but I know I'm completely deaf and blind most of the time. But I believe that every once in a while God gives us a slap upside the head, something with a little more "umph" to try to say, "Pay attention!" That slap takes different forms, depending on what we need at the time and what might actually get our attention. That which means something for you might be completely innocuous to me and vice versa. So much depends on who we are and what speaks to us based on our heritage, our culture, our understanding of and familiarity with cultural mythology and its symbolism.

To wit: I grew up in a conservative Christian milieu with its attendant symbolism of God who took on human form in Jesus Christ. Jesus left the Earth two millennia ago and returned to His Father in heaven, but left us with God's personage in the Holy Spirit who is represented in Christian mythology as a dove. (I certainly don't intend to insult any Christians in my audience; I don't use the word 'mythology' to denigrate Christian belief. Mythology is a meaningful part of culture and a powerful way of transmitting shared beliefs and how we understand our world – physically, emotionally, and spiritually. With that said, I suppose it's obvious that I'm not a literalist when it comes to the Christian Bible or beliefs.)

Which brings me to the afternoon of July 2nd. I had been walking through the Galician countryside, cool and overcast, the scent of eucalyptus and manure and pine sap constantly vying for the attention of my olfactory senses. The sights and sounds and tastes of northwestern Spain drew me constantly closer to the heart of Galicia. I was absorbed in my memories of the previous forty days, missing Maria, wondering and worrying about what was waiting for me on the other side of this bridge, this Camino, and at the same time simply enjoying the moment, if it's possible to do that while also being preoccupied with the past and the future. I should have been feeling calm and confident after receiving dreams of encouragement and seeing and hearing and feeling God dancing in the wind as I walked among wheat fields only a couple of weeks ago. But as I've said, sometimes I'm just not too bright. Clueless at times is how some might describe me and I'd find that description hard to argue with. All those feelings, sights, smells, and sounds I remember as clearly as if I had just experienced them this morning. Here's where, I think, God lost some patience with me and decided He'd better use a more forceful hand to get my attention. I was walking alongside a farm, the path of the Camino meandering among several of its out-buildings, leading me past a mammoth, ancient stone barn, when suddenly and without warning a dove flew out of nowhere, right in front of my face and brushed my forehead directly between the eyes with the tip of its right wing. It took a few seconds to figure out what had happened; I just barely caught a white dove in my peripheral vision as it flew away. All I noticed at the moment was the fluttering of its wings and the brush of its wing tip on my forehead.

One might say, on the one hand, that an albino pigeon with a faulty navigational system had nearly run into me. That's how many, maybe most people would describe the event. On the other hand, the Christian mythological symbol of God's presence on Earth had touched my third eye (if I might be allowed to mix Hindu and Christian symbolism) with its wing just at the moment when I was needing some guidance and a sign that I was truly following God's plan for my life. For me, the latter image, especially given everything else that had happened on the Camino, makes perfect sense. Without this brief, fleeting event the Camino would have been just as meaningful for me. But God knows I'm dense and that sometimes I need that whap upside the head. I believe that on July 2nd, walking through the countryside of Galicia, He chose to give me what he knew I needed.

Chance Meetings?

July 3rd

Two pilgrims at a water fountain near Sarria

Tilly, Katalyn, the two people whose names I embarrassingly can't remember, and I started walking from Gonzar early, if not bright. The weather from here until we got to "the end of the world," Finisterre, would be cloudy and cool for the most part, with brief periods of sun breaks. In contrast, the day I arrived in Finisterre the weather was bright, warm, and sunny – picture perfect, or as my old voice teacher would say, a "Chamber of Commerce day." But until then, our raincoats or ponchos were always ready at the top of our back packs.

We walked through the pueblos of Castromaior, Hospital de la Cruz, Ventas de Narón, Ligonde, Airexe, Avenostre, Palas de Rei, San Xulian y Pontecampaña, Casanova, Loboreiro, and Furelos before finally arriving at Melide. These were all tiny pueblos, about half without a bar (café) or any other place to stop. I could imagine centuries past when these pueblos were, if not thriving, at least populated with many more families who counted the town as home, the next pueblo being populated by "the other people." Even a few kilometers away would have been a walk that wouldn't have been taken without good reason. I've read that in most of the world up until the last century, throughout their entire lives most people never got farther than thirty miles from the place of their birth. I felt that some of the residents of these pueblos might have yet been in that population. As a side note, the reader may have noticed that there have been many pueblos with the word "hospital" in them, which means in Spanish exactly what it does in English. *Hospital de la Cruz* refers to an old hospital, which building, if not the services, still exists at the entrance to the pueblo. Apparently, walking the Camino in centuries past was a much more dangerous and demanding undertaking.

I don't remember which, but in one of the pueblos we were fortunate enough to be treated to free coffee, water, and snacks by a group of volunteers from the Mennonite Church. I had a cup of coffee and asked a woman if there might be a bathroom available. She answered me in Spanish with a distinct American accent. Switching to English, I asked her where she was from and we began talking. Judi was a Mennonite from Virginia and was spending the week in this little pueblo with her husband, Pablo, and other church volunteers to serve the pilgrims who came through. As we talked, I learned that she was currently living and working in Granada, the city to which I planned to go after the Camino to begin my new life in Spain. She and Pablo taught English and worked in other outreach programs through their church. I knew no one in Granada; I had only chosen that city for my new home because I spent three weeks there taking Spanish classes some years earlier and I had thoroughly enjoyed the ambiance of the city, especially the ready availability of flamenco and the history of the city: it was the last region of Spain to be held by the Muslims who had built the Alhambra fortress and the still existing thousand-year-old houses in the *Albaicin*.

The Camino continued to overwhelm me: The day after I had been touched by the wing of a dove I met an American who lived in Granada and offered to help me get settled there. I've mentioned in a previous post that one of the side effects of Prozac withdrawal is lack of control of the tear ducts and I have to admit that I had a difficult time talking with Judi as I was struck, yet again, by another miracle. I didn't get to meet Pablo that day, but she gave me their phone number and a standing invitation to dinner when I arrived in Granada. We met up a few weeks later in that city and they became my most helpful and best friends in Spain.

Moving on, I finally arrived in Melide at an utterly unremarkable albergue. Tilly had gone ahead from where I met Judi. I stayed about fifteen minutes to talk and Tilly normally walked faster than I, so I didn't see her until arriving in Melide. I continued walking, though, with Katalyn and the others who I caught up with after a half hour or so of solo sauntering. When we finally arrived, we chose the *Albergue Apalpador* because there were only twelve beds per room, even though it was more expensive, at twelve Euros. One learns quickly that fewer beds per room decreases the statistical probability of having to listen to snoring the entire night. The sleeping situation may have had an advantage over the municipal albergue nearby, but the kitchen was tiny and there was no dining or lounge area. By this time we had become albergue aficionados. Many times, for only five to seven Euros, we had had very comfortable accommodations with lounge areas, dining rooms, washing machines, well-equipped kitchens, and comfortable beds. I suppose our "pilgrim attitudes" had been compromised by too much luxury, relatively speaking. But we made due. We found Tilly after we had checked in. She told me that she had saved a place for me in the other albergue which turned out to be much nicer, but I didn't change my lodging this time. I wish I had.

My guidebook says, loosely translated which is the only way I can do it, that *"[t]he imminence of Santiago lights a wick of anxiousness until it converts the present journey into slow diligent process. From this point to Santiago no large population centers remain, no majestic cathedrals, no important monasteries, but only green hills and small forests that one walks over and through without further digression or detour. The pilgrim is forced south by the numerous rivers of this region when he wants to go directly west to The Ulla River Valley, to Santiago."*

That's all true except the part about a 'wick of anxiousness' being lit. It was more a wick of anxiety. I looked to Santiago with a sense of ambivalence. I wanted to get there, but I didn't. There were those mixed emotions again. The idea of walking the Camino in order to reach a destination, to complete it, had long ago been abandoned. I wanted to see the Cathedral of Santiago, but I didn't want the Camino to end. I wonder if a babe in the womb feels the same way. You have to move on, but the womb of the Camino had been so warm, protective, and comfortable. Maybe comfortable isn't the right word: A baby is cramped in the womb as my feet were cramped in my boots. But everything you need and could possibly want is here, right here every day on the Camino, given to you, pressed down, shaken together, and overflowing. And what's on the other side? Did I really want to know? By this time I had decided to continue walking to Finisterre, so I was able to approach Santiago knowing that the journey was not yet complete; I wasn't going to be forced out of the womb immediately. But I knew that a week in the future I would be at the end, as far as I could walk unless another miracle gave me the ability to continue walking across the Atlantic Ocean. I don't know why I didn't think at the time of turning around and making the return pilgrimage to Montserrat. I wish now that I had.

Salceda

From Melida it's two day's walk to Santiago: Melida to Pedrouzo is 33 Km; Pedrouzo to Santiago is 20.1. This is according to my guide, *El Camino de Santiago* published by Santiana Ediciones Generales,S.L. (I don't know why I didn't mention this earlier. Maybe I was holding off on the important information to see if you'd stay with me this far. This is a guide for the French route, so it was only useful to me from Logroño, where the French Route joins the Catalan, to Santiago. As I mentioned before, the guide that I purchased in Lléida which led me from that city to Logroño was "lost" in the mail.) At any rate, Tilly, Katalyn, and the other people I was walking with decided to change that schedule a little. We stopped in Salceda, rather than walking all the way to Pedrouzo as the guide suggested, then to Monte de Gozo the final night, which is only 4.4 Km from the cathedral in Santiago. This plan had two advantages in our estimation; the route on July 4th was shorter by 8.8 Km, and stopping at Monte de Gozo the night of July 5th gave us another easy day, plus it enabled us to take a short and pleasant walk into Santiago the morning of the 6th. We would then be able to beat the crowds to the pilgrim office to receive our Compostelas, our certificates of completion, and have time to find a pension where we could deposit our back packs and

216

clean up before the Pilgrim Mass which takes place daily at noon at the Cathedral of Santiago.

Courtyard of the albergue/hotel in Salceda

There is only one albergue in Salceda; small, only twelve spaces, but very modern, clean, and comfortable. Unfortunately, and I say that with tongue in cheek, there were only three beds available in the albergue, which Katalyn, Tilly, and the other German girl took. There being no room in the inn, the other man in our group was going to continue walking to the next town, 8.8 Km away, but the wonderful people at the albergue gave him a bed at no charge that was available for hotel staff who might need a place to sleep on occasion at the hotel.

Hotel on the left, albergue at the end of the walk.

Oh, did I mention there was also a hotel on the property? Guess where yours truly slept. Yes, I "took one for the team" and spent the extra money for a king-size bed in a quiet, well-appointed room with a modern, full bathroom and plenty of steaming hot water all to myself.

After a few days walking with people who were speaking German most of the time, my brain, of its own volition it seemed, began digging into its deepest recesses for any remnants of data and information it could retrieve through synapses unused since my freshman and sophomore days in college where I took 2-1/2 semesters of German – one half more than the requirement for music majors. My intentions were good; I wanted to continue studying the language after taking the required two semesters to become fluent enough to read scholarly journals published in German, but we all know what the road to hell is paved with, and the time required for someone who is somewhat less than talented at foreign languages became a luxury I couldn't afford, so I dropped out of the course half way through my 3rd semester. (Interestingly, just last night, as I write this, I dreamed that I was reading a German newspaper and telling someone that I could understand about 75% of what I was reading. That was before composing this post, or even thinking about it. Life is nothing if not strange.) But somewhere, buried deep in my gray matter there still exists a wealth of German vocabulary and grammar. I found that after a few days of being immersed in German conversation, vocabulary I hadn't remembered in over 35 years was coming back to me. I wasn't able to converse with Tilly or Katalyn, but words and phrases would come to me without trying, as random thoughts, unbidden but not unwelcome. I began thinking that perhaps it would be possible for me to return to my study of German, that that may not be a hindrance to my progress in learning Spanish, and that I might even be able to learn Catalan so that I could feel more comfortable in Catalunya, where, even though Castilian is spoken, it's still a foreign language and you're not considered "one of the family" if you don't attempt to learn their language. Since my recent "back on track" dream, I had been thinking that I would return to at least an informal study of music. If I were going to live in Spain, a quick flight to Germany to visit a library or just attend a concert would be a real possibility. Who knows? The possibilities before me were turning from something I vaguely hoped for to something I could reasonably start planning. I felt as if I were awakening from at 35-year coma. It was exciting but I had the vague feeling of, "Where have I been? What's happened to me? Where do I go from here?" I was reminded of a film, *Awakenings*, where people who have lived in a catatonic state in an extended care facility for many years are "awakened" by injections of dopamine. They are suddenly alive, cognizant of themselves and their surroundings. They enjoy life and relationships, they feel happiness, their lives have purpose and meaning again. In short, their humanity is restored. I also remembered that this effect of the dopamine treatment was only temporary. Yin and yang again. Could I avoid their fate?

Back to the Camino and some random notes that I made in my journal: I haven't seen Maria for several days and I fear I have lost touch with her. I have her phone number and I'll probably be able to call her from my phone when I get to Santiago, as it's a large enough city for my fly-by-night carrier to cover. Will she want to see me again? Or were we just *Camino amigos*, camino friends, people you meet while walking, spend a few days or weeks with, and then never see again? I'm also missing my guitar. Well, not so much my guitar, but playing the guitar. OK, to be honest, I'm missing my guitar also – it's a work of art, something I enjoy touching and looking at as much as playing. It was made by José Ruiz Pedregosa of Jaen, Spain. Pedregosa's craftsmanship is distinctive and masterful. I bought the guitar as much for how it looked as for how it sounded. I'm wondering how I can get it sent to Spain: I don't have an address – I'm homeless for all practical purposes.

These and other thoughts fly around and through my head as we walk toward Monte de Gozo on July 5th. The alternating and sometimes mixed scents of eucalyptus and manure waft past me. The cool drizzle of the morning becomes a perfect, warm, partly sunny afternoon. I'm listening to the girls converse among themselves in German, changing to French to talk with the other man in the group who, if I remember correctly, was from Switzerland. They occasionally switch to English to talk with me. Santiago looms ahead and I'm trying to remain happy.

July 5th and 6th. If you'll permit me to relate just one more dream… This one is timeless, as are all dreams that have significance for our lives and our being-ness, but this one more so. *I am sitting comfortably in a room talking with my good friend, Jesus. No, not just any Jesús, but that Jesus – savior, son of man, prince of peace. Just before the dream begins, as the curtain opens so to speak, Jesus has referred to me as "Jesus." The dream begins and, naturally, I ask him,*

221

"Why did you call me Jesus?" He responds, matter-of-factly, *"Because I am in you and you are in me."*

I know what you're thinking; that's just standard Christian philosophy, standard Christian dogma. No big deal. My subconscious mind was probably rehashing a sermon from years ago that got dislodged from some brain cells by too much wine the night before. But there are dreams, and then, there are dreams. Sometimes you awake and know that your dream environment was so surrealistic that it could only have been a dream. I know, surrealistic technically means dream-like, but it's taken on a meaning of "really, really weird and dream-like." This was not one of those. This was one of those dreams where you become aware of being awake without having awoken, when you wonder if it was a dream or if you might have just been in an alternate universe, another existence for a few minutes. My opinion, take it or leave it, is that while my body was sleeping, the real me had a little conversation with Jesus. That's my story and I'm sticking to it.

As I walked the Camino, this dream took on more and more significance. And I've found that this concept is not just Christian dogma, although it was expressed in my case, given to me by The Holy Spirit in Christian terms, because that's what made most sense to me. To others it's given in terms they can understand. In Thomas Merton's book *Mystics and Zen Masters*, he relates how a Zen practitioner might understand the same idea: Speaking of the "void," or better for Western minds, the *pure affirmation of the fullness of positive being*, Merton writes, *"The void...may be said to have two aspects. First, it simply is what it is. Second, it is realized, it is aware of itself, and to speak improperly, this awareness (Prajna/wisdomcontemplation) is 'in us,' or better, we are 'in it.'"* Could one describe the spirit of Jesus as the pure affirmation of the fullness of positive being? I think so.

The last days before Santiago all my experiences, dreams, feelings, desires, fears, in fact, my whole life swirled around me as I walked. I had come to terms with the end of my sojourn along the outskirts of heaven, greatly aided by the thought that after Santiago I still had eighty kilometers' walk to Finisterre ahead of me. And, truth to tell, I wasn't completely moribund, I was still enjoying walking with my new-found German friends, especially Tilly who, even though she didn't feel perfectly comfortable conversing in English (it was, after all, her fourth language), made the effort so that I wouldn't feel completely left out of the German and French conversations going on around me.

The albergue at Monte de Gozo, 4km from Santiago

Our little group stopped for the night, July 5th, in Monte de Gozo at what can only be described as a base camp prepared for at least 400 pilgrims, expandable to 800 during holy years (those in which Saint James' name day falls on the Sabbath). The barracks-style accommodations are comfortable, although the kitchen facilities were a little cramped for such a potentially large accumulation of pilgrims. No matter, we still managed to have a nice pilgrim meal, taking turns with other groups for table and cooking space. If I remember correctly, dinner comprised spaghetti, bread, fruit, and the requisite bottle of wine. Carbohydrates and wine, the stuff of pilgrim sustenance! All pilgrims know, *"¡No hay Camino sin vino!"* (There's no Camino without wine! Sounds better in

Spanish, ¿doesn't it?) The following day, July 6th, we awoke at the usual time, shouldered our packs, and started the short walk into Santiago de Compostela. From Monte de Gozo one only has to walk a half hour to reach the outskirts of the city, and then carefully follow those familiar yellow arrows to the Cathedral of Santiago. The buildings of the city are tall enough to obscure the cathedral and even its steeples, so it's somewhat surprising when you round a corner of a narrow street and find yourself in a large plaza facing the entrance to the cathedral.

Surprise! Here's the cathedral. (And forcing a smile for the camera)

I know, from reading books and travelogues about the Camino that the typical pilgrim feels a mixture of elation and relief at reaching the Cathedral of Santiago de Compostela. One is supposed to experience a great feeling of accomplishment, like conquering Mt. Everest or swimming the English Channel, to feel ecstatic at being able to check off one more item in one's "bucket list." I don't know what my friends were feeling, but I felt numb, completely and utterly numb. It was as if I were holding my Bachelor's Degree of Music in my hands and saying to myself, once again, now what? They say in any undertaking you're supposed to enjoy the journey; not so much the destination. That was my feeling in spades. I had enjoyed the journey; maybe enjoyed it too much. Now that I was at the end, all I wanted was for the journey to continue. I have to admit that I felt childish. After all, isn't an adult supposed to live in the real world of responsibilities, deadlines, mortgage payments, work: the daily grind? I had, perhaps, enjoyed the life of the Camino too much the last several weeks without all that, living again as a child: No responsibilities, no deadlines, no mortgage or even rent payments, and my only work was carrying a back pack through some of the most beautiful country imaginable, walking and talking with interesting people from around the world, and at the end of each day relaxing, eating, drinking and then sleeping like a baby in preparation for the next day where I'd do it all again, anticipating the coming day with its sights and sounds and smells and cafes and bars and more time to do nothing but contemplate my existence or just clear my mind and enjoy life as the beautiful scenery of Northern Spain came at me at a leisurely, walking pace.

An Ecstatic Reunion

July 6th, 8:30 AM

There I was, forty-seven days after climbing through wind and rain to reach the monastery at Montserrat, now standing in front of The Cathedral of Santiago de Compostela, having walked nearly the entire breadth of Northern Spain. I should have felt happy. I should have felt elated. I should have felt a sense of accomplishment and pride.

I felt let down, directionless.

For the last 8 years I had had a goal: To walk the Camino de Santiago. I read the books, planned what I'd need, lived in anticipation of the day I'd arrive in Spain with my backpack and boots and begin the adventure. And the adventure had been more than I could possibly have expected or even could have dreamed. I lived each day on the Camino simply sensing life. It sounds a little trite, but it's the best way I can describe the experience of walking – sauntering as Thoreau would put it – seeing the countryside as it passed by me, feeling the heat of the sun in Catalunya and Aragon, the rain in Galicia, the wind across the *meseta*. I tasted *pulpo* in Galicia and the best fish stew I've ever had in Villafranca Montes de Oca. I heard everything from vespers in Montserrat to the still silence of walking through farmlands, broken only by the sound of cow bells and occasional bleating of sheep, to the overwhelming

228

cacophonous noise of thousands of trucks and cars almost bumper to bumper at 100 kilometers per hour as if they were one, long train speeding by me only an arm's length away as I walked along a highway after finding myself lost in the Aragon desert and trying to find my way back to the Camino. I smelled eucalyptus forests, fresh-mown hay, newly plowed fields and I believe I even smelled the water in the irrigation canals encircling them. Even through the discomfort of my painful feet I felt the energizing endorphins created by the constant physical exertion of walking all day, every day. I had left my last bottle of Prozac at the foot of the cross at the *Cruz de Fierro* and felt immeasurably better without them than I had ever felt with.

And here I was at the end of all that, in Santiago, staring at the cathedral and wondering what to do next.

"Well, suck it up, pilgrim," I thought to myself. "The opera ain't over 'till the fat lady sings, and the fat lady is still waiting for me in Finisterre, 80 kilometers down the road." After Finisterre I would go to Granada. And hadn't I already met someone who would help me get settled there? Is the hand of God not directing my steps?

So, first things first. After walking an hour the first thing you do is eat breakfast, which is exactly what my little group and I did. We found a bar near the cathedral and I had my usual *desayuno de peregrino: café con leche* with a croissant. I added to it fresh squeezed orange juice which was the norm in Spain. Some restaurants served frozen orange juice at a lesser price if you ask for it, but in almost all of them you'll find a juice machine and a stack of oranges right next to the espresso maker. If you order orange juice, it will be squeezed from fresh oranges while you watch.

The entrance to the pilgrim office in Santiago

I waited until 9:00 or shortly thereafter when the pilgrim office opened so I could register and receive the Compostela, the certificate showing that one has walked the Camino de Santiago. The rest of the group stayed in the bar; I just wanted to get the registration process over with, find a pension, and get rid of my back pack. I was early so the line was short. I've been told that at times, during the busier times of the year the line can wind down the stairs, through the courtyard outside the office doors, and into the street. Leaving the office, someone handed me a small flyer advertising a nearby pension. I asked him if the pension was open at this time of day. I wanted to check in if possible and rid myself of my back pack. He told me that it was still too early, but he took me there himself and found the owner who allowed me to check in anyway. Ah, the joys of capitalism: Even though it was hours before normal check-in time, he had a room, I had money, we made an exchange and both of us were better off than we had been only minutes before. I suppose the fact that he knew there were plenty of other pensions and hostels available gave him incentive to allow me an early check in.

The rest of the morning I wandered around Santiago, in and out of narrow streets that had been there for over a thousand years and had seen hundreds of thousands of pilgrims before me.

It was close to noon when the daily pilgrim mass started at the cathedral. I hadn't attended mass since Zaragoza and I wouldn't miss this one for the world. I found my traveling companions and we went into the cathedral at about 11:30, maybe even a little earlier to make sure we got a seat. Even at this time of the year, not the high season for pilgrims, the cathedral was completely filled to standing room only by the time mass started. I understood very little of what the priest was saying; my grasp of Spanish is just not nearly good enough to filter out the pronounced echo of the cathedral combined with the rapid-fire delivery of the Ordinary of the Mass. And, even though the priest delivered the homily in, alternately, Spanish, French, German, and English, with the echo and miscellaneous noises that necessarily emanate from a thousand people, I didn't even understand the English parts. It didn't matter though; the feeling couldn't have been more powerful. Everything, from the *Kyrie* to the *Agnus Dei* and finally the swinging of the *botafumeiro*, the giant incense burner, seemed to overwhelm all my senses. Even the crowds of tourists couldn't reduce the holy effect.

Waiting for the Pilgrim Mass to begin in the Cathedral of Santiago

And my cathedral experience was not over. As if the music and incense and the feeling of receiving the ultimate blessing to my seven weeks on the Camino were not enough, as I stood in the pew, waiting to exit the cathedral after Mass, I saw Maria on the other side of the cathedral. She was looking at me as I looked at her through the crowd. I saw her as if she were the only other person in the cathedral. As the crowds shuffled along toward the cathedral exits I lost sight of her but found her again near the huge doors at the rear of the cathedral. We hugged as if we were long lost friends and she told me that her heart skipped a beat when she saw me. Hearing that caused my heart to skip several beats. To say I had missed her the last several days doesn't even begin to describe my feelings, and to hear her say anything that would indicate she had missed me also, after the experience of the Mass, and the emotional roller coaster of the last several days was an overpowering emotional experience. I thought I was used to one miracle after another but I was inundated with emotion yet again.

We spent the rest of the day together wandering around Santiago, doing the "tourist thing." It was cool and rain threatened, so I bought a thick, heavy, hooded sweatshirt that had a University of Santiago logo in it – something completely unsuited to backpacking across the country. But I was almost at the end and I'd find room in my pack for the remaining 80 Km to Finisterre for the comfort of a warm sweatshirt to get me around Santiago de Compostela.

I had already paid for my pension so I slept there that night, but the following day I moved to the pension where Maria was staying. Being in the same pension was more convenient for making arrangements for our outings around the town and had the added benefit of being quieter and more modern at the same price. Oh yeah, I was also right next door to Maria. If for nothing else, that alone made me happy.

Maria had planned to stay a couple of days and then catch a flight back to Barcelona, but I encouraged her – better, pleaded with – to walk to Finisterre with me. I told her that I saw the walk to Finisterre as the coda to a symphony. We had walked the symphony, but without the coda to Finisterre, the piece was incomplete. (I probably came up with that after a bottle of wine.) Fortunately for me, her other Catalunyan friends were also planning to walk to the coast, so, regardless of my lame metaphor, she agreed to go with me. We planned to stay a day in Santiago to rest and leave on the third day, but the night before we intended to start for Finisterre we were out on the town with other Camino amigos and didn't get back to the pension until somewhere between 3:00 and 4:00 in the morning – a typical Spanish pub crawl as we'd done in Burgos. So we stayed another day to recuperate.

That day, the day before we left for Finisterre, Maria took a nap while I went for a walk around town. I had written some

234

post cards to friends and family, including one to Annick, the woman from France we'd walked with for a couple of weeks. I found a post box and as I prepared to put her card in it, I re-read what I had written and thought about Annick and the time we spent walking the Camino, said a brief prayer for her, and then dropped the post card in the box. I continued walking and came to a plaza where I saw, much to my surprise, Beth. She hadn't been walking with Maria the last week or so; they had become separated and lost touch with each other. I had a brief conversation with her, told her that I was planning to walk on to Finisterre and wished her well. On the way back I ran into Lluis and some of his friends whom I had walked with off and on from near the Cruz de Fierro. My little walk around town had become like a mini family reunion. I was very happy to see them and greeted Lluis with a warm, two-handed hand-shake. I found out that Lluis and the others had been walking with Maria pretty regularly the last week or so after I had become separated from her. They asked how Maria was and I told them she was taking a much needed siesta and other small talk, including our plans to leave the next morning for Finisterre.

I returned to the pension, finding that Maria had awoken by this time. She told me she had had a vivid dream during her nap. She told me that she dreamed of Annick, whom she hadn't thought of since we left Burgos. Then she dreamed that I was talking with Beth, and finally that Lluis and I were talking with each other as old friends, and she saw, in her dream, that we shook hands with a two-handed hand shake and talked about the route to Finisterre. By this time in my Camino, none of this surprised me.

The Cathedral of Santiago at night

Finisterre (pt. 1)

July 8th

On July 8th we sallied forth, as Don Quixote, my favorite literary character would say. The weather was overcast and cool, but dry. I had spent a couple of relaxing and enjoyable days in Santiago with Maria. We had become "regulars" in a bar next to the cathedral, if such a thing can happen in that short period of time (with Maria it can and does – she's an instant friend to all who meet her), walking through every street of the *Casco Viejo*, the old part of town, browsing the tourist shops, the open air market, and of course, touring the cathedral and paying homage to the bones of St. James, or Santiago as he's known in these environs, in their silver casket. I didn't attend another Mass, but I took the opportunity daily in the cathedral to pray the rosary I had carried with me across Spain. I'm not a "church goer," and I don't subscribe to a lot of the dogma and ritual of the Catholic Church, but I find praying the rosary to be a kind of meditation. I suppose everyone who meditates finds it difficult to control their wandering mind. For me, the prayers of the rosary and just the physical act of holding the beads and the cross allow me to concentrate and focus my attention.

Leaving Santiago de Compostela on the Camino to Finisterre

I only made one entry in my journal after arriving in Santiago de Compostela, and absolutely no notes in the small guidebook that directed us from Santiago to Finisterre. What little I wrote isn't relevant here, so everything I write about the walk to Finisterre and beyond is from memory, and, as this all occurred almost a year ago, all I have left is vague pictures and impressions combined with strong and emotive feelings I still can't shake.

The walk was peaceful again; the pilgrims, the "day-trippers" who had joined us for the last 100 km to Santiago were gone. Even most of the long distance pilgrims to Santiago were gone; only the hard core pilgrims walked to Finisterre or

Muxia, the ultimate destination. We walked off and on with another group of pilgrims from Catalunya who had become Maria's friends and all spoke, naturally, Catalan among themselves most of the day, Maria included. When I conversed with Maria we spoke in Castilian, and she tried to keep me up to date with the conversation, interpreting for me in Castilian (Spanish to the non-Catalan world), but I had reached the saturation point where a combination of mental and psychological exhaustion seemed to create a stone wall around me and nothing I heard was making much sense. I was also nearing the real end of my Camino and I think I was starting to separate myself, psychologically and emotionally, from people and an environment that I knew I would have to leave behind. I remember stopping at a bar for lunch. The Catalunyans were laughing and enjoying themselves and I was feeling like an outsider. No matter, really. I didn't expect them to all speak in a foreign language all the time just for me. But I tried to order a second beer, a simple thing by this time. I made the request of the bar tender, who looked at me as I ordered but made no attempt to acknowledge my request. I waited. I waited some more. I waited a little longer, finally giving up, leaving angrily without the second beer I really didn't need anyway. Was my Spanish still that bad that he didn't understand me? Or was I not assertive enough to order a beer in Spain? Did the bartender see that I was a foreigner and think it was funny to just mess with me? Maria told me later, when I talked about this with her, that the bartender was just playing *mala folla* to the hilt and said that I shouldn't let it bother me. But it did, nonetheless.

A day or two later, after breakfast in a crowded bar at an albergue, we were all trying to finish preparations for the day and hit the road. I was pulling up the rear, standing at the bar with a 5 euro note in my raised hand, waiting for the bartender/waiter to take my money so I could leave. There were a lot of other people there, all pilgrims, naturally, ordering juice and croissants and *café con leche* and whatever else was available, so the bartender was busy. I was trying to be polite, knowing that he could see me – I was standing practically right in front of him – and it was obvious that I wanted to pay my bill. But he ignored me. My other traveling companions, including Maria were already out the door so I finally raised my voice above the din and told the bartender I'd like to pay.

This is just the way it is in Spain. I'm used to restaurant employees wanting to be paid, understanding that the exchange of money is their *raison d'etre*: when a customer wants to give you money and leave, making room for more paying customers, you take his money, dammit! But an American has to learn to be more assertive in Spain. At least, a non-assertive American – for which I am the *primo* example – has to learn that.

I left feeling frustrated and foolish, feeling that Maria was losing patience with me, which made me feel worse. I spent

240

most of that day walking alone. I needed some time to think, away from Catalan, away from people, away from Maria. The real end of the Camino was staring me in the face and I had no idea what was coming. I had faith that it would all work out, but I felt as if I were in the boat and Jesus was telling me to step out into the sea. Sure, I could see that He's being borne up by the water, but I just didn't feel ready to take that step. Call me faithless, but I was scared to death.

Nearing the ocean

I could also see that my relationship with Maria *was* going, and if fact, *could* go nowhere. To this day I don't know what she saw in me, but it was certainly not anything on which to build a romantic relationship. I had deep admiration and respect for her from the beginning, and over the weeks, that had turned into a lot more, something where it was easy for me to imagine a life-long relationship. But she told me in so many words that she did not want a serious relationship with me or anyone else. It was clear that our relationship had been asymmetrical; her desires and mine not coming from the same place, nor going in the same direction. She told me that she didn't want to rely on anyone for anything and didn't want anyone to rely on her. I told her that sounded great to me; I just wanted to be with her, and not even all the time – just most of the time. I was happy to let her have all the alone time she wanted because I needed that too. Usually, but not always, I managed to maintain an arm's-length friendship.

No matter now. I'm here, she's there. Letting go was difficult. It still is.

We arrived in Finisterre on July 11th. The weather was perfect – warm, sun shining, a perfect beach day. We took off our hiking boots, rolled up our pants, and walked along the shore of the Atlantic Ocean at Finisterre, the end of the known world when it received its name. Later, we checked into the final albergue to drop off our backpacks and Maria changed into a swim suit so she could lie on the beach to soak up the sun. I didn't have a swim suit, but lying on the beach doesn't hold much interest for me anyway. I just took a long, barefoot walk looking for scallop shells, the symbol of the Camino, which were surprisingly difficult to find. Shells of every other type were numerous, but that famous scallop shell was elusive. I finally found a few small ones and gave all but one to Maria. The one I kept for my own souvenir, fortunately, didn't get sent back to the States later, where it probably would have been lost to post office thieves.

Arriving in Finisterre

Finisterre (pt. 2)

The remainder of the daylight hours we wandered the town and ran into others whom we had walked with at various stages of the Camino and had arrived in Finisterre with us. We ate at a café overlooking a beautiful harbor, just sitting and talking, waiting for the sun to set.

The café where we had wine and tapas, overlooking the harbor in Finisterre.

There is a tradition among pilgrims who walk all the way to Finisterre: to walk to the lighthouse in the early evening and watch the sun sink into the Atlantic Ocean. I suppose a purist would have walked out to the lighthouse, about three kilometers distance from the albergue, but the purist also walks in sack cloth and ashes, barefoot, carrying only a gourd for water and begs for food and lodging along the way. I had eschewed the purist pilgrimage before I even started. Hadn't I already taken a cab once before? What was one more little ride? I didn't have to twist Maria's arm to get her to agree to a cab, and we arrived at the lighthouse about an hour before sunset. The sky was partly cloudy, but that just gave the sun something to light up as it descended over the horizon and made the scene that much more resplendent. There were others making the ritual funeral pyre for a piece of clothing or pair of boots; another pilgrim tradition. I had already left two shirts along the way that I didn't need and had sent back to the States a pair of shoes that I had outgrown during the first half of the Camino, so I had nothing left to burn. I enjoyed their offerings to the Camino vicariously. Maria had already found a place to sit on the rocks to watch the sunset and was looking at the sea as I was enjoying the fire and talking with some other people. I went to the lighthouse café (naturally, with all those people there every night of the Spring, Summer, and Fall months, there's going to be someone to sell food and drink) and got a couple of cups of white wine (Styrofoam, unfortunately – no glass allowed outside) and took them out to where Maria was sitting. She had found a very comfortable place to sit – for one.

Maria at the Atlantic Ocean in Finisterre

I asked if she'd mind moving if I could find a comfortable place for two. She was amenable, so I began crawling over rocks, my wine balanced precariously in my hand, trying, successfully, not to spill any. I found the perfect spot, closer to the ocean, further out on the rocks, a place any self-respecting mountain goat could walk to with ease, but completely *loco* in Maria's estimation. She joined me anyway and we sat in silence as the sun sank into the West.

And now I arrive at the point where words fail me. Today, as I write this, is June 29th, 2013, almost a year after I was sitting on the rocks at the coast of Spain; the culmination of an 850-mile pilgrimage. My fingers are on the keyboard of my laptop, but they refuse to move except to say I don't know what to write. But I can't bring you this far and then leave you with such a lousy ending. It would be like that symphony without the coda or leaving off the *denouement* of the murder mystery. Or, do I flatter myself? Does anyone, other than I, really care how it all ended? You've been with me this far. I'll have to take that on faith that you want to hear the end.

So many thoughts vied for attention as I sat staring at the setting sun that they all became like white noise. There was the memory of my sore feet, of perfect peace walking across the *Meseta*, of standing in the cool shower of the irrigation sprayers in the desert of Aragon, of constant snoring in the albergues every night since Logroño in parallel with the memory of having quiet albergues all to myself through Catalunya and Aragon, of frustration with not being able to communicate as well as I'd like but being happy with the progress I'd made in my grasp of Spanish, of elation when remembering Maria saying her heart skipped a beat when she saw me in the cathedral after the feeling of loss as she walked away in Sarria. I thought of Debussy and the sea of wheat and then the music came to me again as I looked at the sea of water before me. I thought of my past, before the Camino, and my future, after the Camino and tried to ignore all that and concentrate on the present: the setting sun in front of me and Maria beside me. My life appeared before me as a blackboard filled with calculus equations, and I know nothing of calculus. I'd come to the Camino to find God. I don't know if I found God, but I had lost myself.

The sun descended though the clouds. The sky on the horizon turned imperceptibly from light blue to orange to red, then faded as the sun sank farther into the sea and finally turned a dark blue. The colors of everything around me washed out as my little part of the Earth turned farther away from the sun, everything around me turning darker and darker shades of gray while the sky turned the deep violet blue and then black of night.

Clambering over rocks a hundred feet above the Atlantic Ocean in daylight seemed like a much better idea than trying to climb back over them in the dark. At least we didn't have to be concerned with spilling our wine. We made it safely back to the lighthouse and walked, flashlight in hand, back to the albergue, mostly in silence.

The next day brought rain and cool air. We took the first bus back to Santiago from where Maria caught a flight to Barcelona. A quick, barely perceptible hug and she was on the bus. She said she didn't like long goodbyes. I guess not. I waited a couple of hours at the bus station, then caught an overnight bus to Granada, the next *etapa,* the next stage of my life's Camino.

Part Three: Postlude

Granada

July 13th, late morning. Granada bus station.

In Santiago, Montse, a fellow pilgrim and new friend, had given me the name of a youth hostel in Granada and had even gone so far as to call them for me to make a reservation. I still hadn't much confidence in my Spanish language abilities so I was grateful for the help to ensure that I had no misunderstandings concerning availability, arrival date, price, and location. The hostel is near the Cathedral of Granada, so I easily found the city bus that would take me near my next stop, *Funky Granada*.

What, you may ask, is a 55-year-old man doing in a youth hostel named, very appropriately, *Funky Granada*? I wondered that myself. I'd be lying if I said I didn't feel out of place, but feeling out of place is something that you have to get accustomed to when traveling or embarking on a new life. The hostel staff was friendly and very helpful, even indulging me in my attempt to communicate in Spanish, only breaking into English when it was absolutely apparent that I was becoming hopelessly lost in translation. *Funky Granada* is a clean, well run, and inexpensive place to stay for a couple of nights. I was assigned a room of two bunk beds, sharing a refrigerator and cook top stove with another room of equal size on the other side of a door that separated the two rooms.

The bathroom that the two rooms shared was clean with a window to the courtyard for ample ventilation and light. One floor up, on the third floor, fourth if counting American style, was a patio with tables and chairs for outdoor dining, although July in Andalucía is only amenable to enjoying the outdoors in early morning and late evening.

Even at 21 euros a night, cheap by tourist standards, I was feeling financially strapped. My money situation was already getting tight after over-spending my budget on the Camino and I needed to immediately cut my expenses to the bone, so I set about finding an inexpensive apartment. Given the poor economic situation of Spain, and the fact that I had arrived in Granada in July when the university students are away, the only difficulty in finding a suitable arrangement was figuring out where I wanted to live, making the phone calls in Spanish to arrange viewing, and then finding the apartment amidst the winding medieval streets of Granada.

Near the room I rented in the Jewish museum in Granada

Out away from the old part of the city there are plenty of high-rise apartment buildings, but I wasn't interested in living in one of those. I constrained my search to the *Albaicin* and the *Barrio Realejo*, the first being the old Muslim quarater across the *Rio Darro* from the Alhambra, the latter being the old Jewish quarter just to the south of it. After only two days of looking I decided on a room on the top floor of an ancient house that was now a Jewish museum on *Cuesta Rodrigo del Campo*, only about 15 minutes' walk from the Alhambra. Inside the walls surrounding the house there were two gardens, one of which was outside the window of my room, with grape arbors, orange and lemon trees, and a fountain. There were two other rooms for rent on my floor, currently vacant, but eventually I'd have to share the kitchen and bathroom with two other tenants. As this was summer, and university was not in session, I had the whole floor to myself.

The fountain in the garden outside my room

I had called Judi, whom I met on the Camino and mentioned in an earlier chapter, and her husband, Pablo, as soon as I arrived in Granada and arranged to meet them for coffee and *churros* at a café near the cathedral. They told me about *Totes y Amigos*, a bar where people met twice a week for *intercambio* (interchange) to practice English and Spanish, as appropriate, where I was to spend most Tuesday and Thursday evenings. (Sadly, Totes has retired and the bar has been sold. I don't know if the new owners are maintaining the *intercambio* tradition. I doubt they are, as it was common for many people to come and take table space and talk for two hours and only order one or two drinks. It was great for the patrons, but I don't see how Totes made any money on the deal.) Pablo and Judi also invited me to their apartment for dinner a few times where I met friends of theirs – some Spaniards and some, like themselves, from the States, following the path of service that Jesus had shown them. Pablo and Judi became my best friends and instant support group in Granada. A nicer couple you'll never meet. Pablo even loaned me his guitar for a couple of weeks so I could get back to practicing while waiting for mine to arrive from the States. Of all my memories of Granada, spending time with Pablo and Judi remain some of my fondest.

My plan, financially, was to tutor students of English, so I began putting up flyers advertising my services among the countless others advertising the same thing. As in so many endeavors in life and business, timing is everything. I had arrived in Granada in the middle of July, when the university students are gone and, for the most part, life seems to pause for the summer. Unfortunately, I had also just about run my bank account to zero. Except for a car payment I had no debts, but I *did* have the car payment, no income, and I owed more on my car than it was worth, so I had no choice but to continue making loan payments. I began taking cash advances on my credit cards to pay living expenses – never a good option. I had hoped that that would be temporary, but as July turned into August, and August turned into September, and I had found only one student – for conversation practice only at 5 euros an hour – it became apparent that I was on a trajectory to severe financial hardship, if not absolute ruin. In the meantime, I was trying to live on faith. I was a stranger in a strange land. I had no idea what each day would bring, but hoped for phone calls from prospective students, and tried to fill my days with learning the lay of the land and figure out what I could do to fill each day without spending any more money than necessary.

The view from a patio on the top floor of the museum.

My main objective, outside of finding English students, was to find an authentic (read: non-tourist) Flamenco *tablau*. Sadly, I never found it during my short stay in Granada. There are some good performers at *Le Chien Andalou*, just up the street from the *Plaza Nueva*, but the venue is too close to a hotspot for tourists. I heard some excellent *tocaores* (guitarists) and *cantaores* (singers) there, and saw some very good *bailaroas* (dancers), but the audience was distracting; one time filled with children that ruined the atmosphere to the point where I had to leave only thirty minutes into the show.

On another occasion, I attended a flamenco performance which was part of a series of flamenco concerts through the summer given in the courtyard of an ancient municipal building. After the show I went to a tiny bar nearby and had the good fortune to meet some other people who had been at the concert, and talk with them about flamenco. One was an older gypsy gentleman who owned a bar in the Albaicin, one of the famous "caves" where flamenco performances are held nightly for the tourists. He told me that if I were to come up to the area after 2:00 AM and just hung around and listened I would find the "jam sessions" where I could hear very good music and see some real dancing. Sadly, I didn't take advantage of his advice. I thought I had plenty of time, but the end of my Spanish experience came suddenly.

The effects of what I've previously referred to as PTSD were beginning to show themselves. I've read of people who have had "near death experiences," which seem to me to be better described as actual "death and resuscitation experiences." Those who experienced the other side and then come back often feel out of place, disoriented, incredibly sad to the point of depression. Their life may seem pointless, without purpose. They don't interact comfortably with others; society seems foreign and not understandable. That is *exactly* how I felt, and still feel. As much as I tried to continue with my life, to look at the Camino as a learning and growing experience, I found it difficult to relate to my current reality. For years, ever since my three-week Spanish course in 2006, I had wanted to move to Granada, to live here. Now I was here and I felt out of place and without purpose. I didn't want to return to the States where I have felt a foreigner for many years, but I felt just as foreign here in Granada, and the feeling had nothing to do with the language or culture. I felt like a foreigner vis-a-vis other humans. At *Totes y Amigos* I had met Derek Dohren, a man I had a lot in common with and author of *The Cats of the River Darro*. His life experience, work, marriage, divorce, finances, and so much more seemed to parallel my life in so many ways. He was now living in Granada as an English teacher and author. He introduced me to the head of the school where he was teaching and I went through the motions of giving her my resume, even though I was an American and I knew what that meant for my chances of securing legitimate employment in a language school in Andalucia. Derek is an EU citizen with the legal right to work in Spain. I, sadly, am not and it looked like finding work was going to be an impossibility, at least, finding work that would sustain me financially before my money ran out and my credit cards were charged to the max.

My writing desk, my Camino journal, a glass of wine, and an extra chair – just in case I had a visitor.

I wanted to stay in Granada. I remembered the dream I had on the Camino where I was sure I was told that I was on the right track. I also remembered another dream, one that had followed the one I described earlier, where I was showing a friend around my mother's property in a horse-drawn carriage and telling her that there were two wolves on my mother's property that I had to deal with. That dream was less definite in meaning to me, but no less important in my estimation. The fact that it followed the "music" dream seemed to have importance, but I didn't know how to interpret it. (Wouldn't it be nice to have a Joseph hanging around for just such an occasion?) Still, I wondered if I were doing the right thing, would I feel so out of place. Was the feeling purely attributable to my own brand of PTSD, or were my guardian angels telling me something?

After seven weeks in Granada, I made the difficult decision to return to the States, find work, pay off all debt, and save everything possible for another "attempt at the summit." This was about one week after receiving, and paying the shipping and customs duties for all the possessions I'd need for my new life in Spain: clothing, English language teaching books, and my guitar. I thought it ironic (is that the right word?) that I'd paid U.S. import duties on the guitar that I bought from the guitar maker in Jaen, Spain when I had it imported to the States, then had to pay import duties on it when I had it shipped back to Spain. That's government, I guess. They get you coming and going. I read Derek's book and admired his persistence, remaining in Granada after his money had run out, having to live with friends and work through an incredibly difficult time financially. But I had to be honest and realistic with myself: Derek had the legal right to live and work in Spain. I was an illegal alien. His family was an inexpensive flight of a few hours away; mine was a $1500 ticket and 15 hours of flying in addition to ground transportation. My mother is not young and I knew that there was a real possibility I would have to make the trip to the States at a moment's notice. I have two unmarried children, but they are both of marrying and child-bearing age. What would I do if circumstances required that I return to see them? All these thoughts weighed on my mind as I watched my financial position wither to nothing.

If I had enough faith I suppose I could have lived here. I would like to think that I can live on faith alone, but even after all the experiences of the Camino, I'm not there yet. *The lilies of the field grow and they neither toil nor spin, and the birds of the air neither sow nor reap nor store away in barns.* Who am I to consider tomorrow or what happens to my mother or children?

But I do. Again, my lack of faith reared its ugly head and I bought a ticket for a flight to the States. I felt sick. Defeated. Like the person who attempts to swim the English Channel and, half way across, decides it's too difficult and turns around. But maybe, just maybe, God gave me the gift of discernment. Maybe I did the right thing in returning, to rebuild my finances and prepare for the next pilgrimage and a return to Spain and Granada with enough money to survive and pay for unexpected events that are sure to arise. I've been able to help my mother and my children since I've been back. I don't know if I was able to keep the wolves from my mother's door, but there were two occasions where the purpose of that dream may have been fulfilled while I lived with her upon returning and while looking for employment. I've almost completed my plans for the next pilgrimage from Barcelona to Rome, and, *Dios quiere*, God willing, in ninety-one weeks from this writing I'll again see my employer's office complex in my rear-view mirror and be on my way to the next adventure.

God willing.

Esperando: Waiting. Hoping.

So, what did it all mean? I still haven't figured that out. I imagine I'll be lying on my death bed still wondering. Truth is, I think we waste a lot of time searching for meaning. A tragedy happens – the death of a child, cancer, an airplane explodes over Scotland. What does it mean?

Maybe, as Forest Gump said, "It happens," or, as the reporter trying to keep up with him transformed it, "Shit happens." That's the world we live in.

But otherworldly, unimaginable, unfathomable good happens also: Finding sixteen dollars laying on the ground when you have to take your daughter to the doctor and didn't, until just then, even have the money to pay for parking; having a little chat with Jesus during the night; fifty days of incredible, other-worldly peace, contentment, and happiness between Montserrat and Finisterre.

Maybe it's a Zen thing: asking for the meaning of tragedy or beauty is an invalid question. Just as well, ask, "Is it as hot in the summer as it is in Chicago?"

We experience good and bad and everything in between. Better than look for meaning is to relish the experience, learn from it and grow into something different from what we were before.

As I walked just this side of heaven, with all the wonderful experiences and feelings, enjoying the interaction with other pilgrims from every part of the world, enjoying *pulpo* and the joy of a frigid beer in the shade from a 100-degree sun, relishing the freedom from computers, telephones, deadlines, deliverables, and the virtual chain to a desk in a cubicle, still my feet ached like a son-of-a-bitch every single day on the Camino and I was incredibly frustrated by my lack of communication abilities. It may seem that there is no perfection, but as a Zen master might say, or at least I would say, in imperfection there is perfection. Everything contains yin and yang. In all things there is a balance. Walking on the border of heaven, I was still "grounded" in every sense of the word. My aching feet reminded me that I was still a slave to gravity; I was still Earthbound and dependent on my physical body as much as I was having a heavenly experience and enjoying the fruits of the spirit more than I ever had, or even thought possible.

I had wandered in the desert of Aragon, having lost my way with a guidebook I couldn't completely understand. I had discovered sights, sounds, flavors, smells, and sensations I never knew existed. I limped into Lleída literally cursing my feet. I had felt freedom, liberty, and ultimate happiness. I had felt extreme frustration at not being able to communicate to a bartender that I would like another beer or just, please, take my money so I can pay my bill and get back on the Camino.

I had fallen in love. I had lost love. I had walked between Heaven and Earth. Yin and yang. Perfect balance.

And for a month I was given the gift of getting to know a woman with a kind, generous, uplifting, energy-inducing spirit. I haven't corresponded or talked with Maria for several months and may not see her again. But the fact that we don't have an on-going relationship now does not detract from the extra magic that I experienced on the Camino because of her presence. The chapter entitled, "Maria," when I originally posted the rough draft on the blog site that was the basis for this memoir, had the title "A Hymn to a Saint." Later, I thought that title may be just a little over the top. I was sure Maria would vehemently disagree with my assessment of her and it would probably embarrass her if she were ever to read the blog post or this memoir. So I changed it. But now I'm not so sure that "saint" is hyperbole. There are various meanings for that word, and there are various levels of sainthood. One definition of saint is "a person of great holiness, virtue, or benevolence." In my experience, admittedly short, that definition describes Maria to a T. I readily admit that I allowed my feelings to expand past that of pure respect and admiration and fantasized, on occasion, about a life with her after the Camino. But a year later, putting the whole experience into context, I think meeting Maria and spending a month with her was just another gift of the Camino, one more facet of a life-changing experience.

I want nothing more than to experience all this again, but I fear that if I attempt another pilgrimage I won't have the same, or even an equivalent experience and the disappointment will kill me. Was it Jesus or Paul who said, "You fear because you lack faith."? It's true. I do lack faith. I'm no different from the Jews wandering the desert. Even after the miracles shown them by God, still they looked away and worshipped the golden calf. Likewise, after being literally touched by a dove, I wonder if I should step out of the boat and into the sea. I fear the future.

As a way to keep my goal in front of me and maintain some small sense of sanity as I wait, I have created a countdown calendar, like an advent calendar, the difference being, rather than counting days, there is only one page per week to count down the time until I get to leave my job and start my next pilgrimage to Rome: Ninety weeks to go as of this writing. On each page, each week, I have printed a saying that gives me something to think about throughout the week. I searched books and the web to find sayings that I thought might be appropriate. On one page is a saying I found on a site of Zen koans and philosophy:

> *Before enlightenment I chopped wood and carried water.*
> *After enlightenment I chopped wood and carried water.*

When I first saw that I fixed on the ending of the pair of sentences, "…chopped wood and carried water," and understood that to mean that life continues regardless of who we are, what we do, what we've experienced, or what we've accomplished. We may learn, or not. We may grow, or not. We may change, or not. But whatever we do, whatever happens to us, whoever we are, mundane life continues. We have to work, to make a living, to produce at least as much as we consume. There is no out, no alternative, no existence outside of this earthly, physical life for as long as we are here. One can experience the best that God has to offer or suffer the worst the devil can dish out, and still, one must continue to chop wood and carry water.

Recently, after having written a good deal of what I remember from my experience walking from Montserrat to Finisterre, I have reinterpreted those sentences. Yes, before the Camino I chopped wood and carried water and after the Camino I still chop wood and carry water. But, and this makes all the difference, there is a trick of language in those two sentences. They appear to be parallel and congruent, equal except for the first word in each: "I". But "I" is only a metaphor, a sound, an utterance that stands for the subject of the sentence, which is an image or idea created by the mind. Is the subject the same in each sentence? Grammatically, yes. In reality, no. Before and after enlightenment, before and after the Camino, the real question is, does the "I" in the two sentences refer to the same person?

271

I propose to the reader that the person chopping wood and carrying water before the Camino is not the same as the person after. The meaning of the sentences is hiding in the noun which is really a verb; an action word. The stasis in the identical metaphorical subject implied in these two, short sentences hides the true meaning. Mundane life continues but it is experienced in completely different ways by different people. Those different people might inhabit the same body, looking like the same person. But before enlightenment and after, before the experience of the Camino and after, they are not the same person.

I wouldn't presume that everyone was, is, will be changed by the Camino experience, but it is certainly possible and in my case it was a certainty. After all I've thought and written I still can't put into words how I am different, how I've changed, but I have. I don't see anything the same way as I did before. I don't react to anything in the same way. My desires, hopes, and dreams have morphed into something, in some cases slightly, in others radically different.

So, I'll make another pilgrimage, walking in faith. I may not get lost in the desert. I may not experience new sights, sounds, flavors, and smells. I will not find another Maria. But I will experience and find whatever God has in store for me. And afterwards, yet again, I will not be I.

Gratitude

Thank you for purchasing and reading this memoir of what was for me a powerful experience. Everyone walks their own camino through life and if your camino leads you to the one in Spain, then I hope that your experience is as meaningful for you as mine was for me. If you choose to take that little saunter, please keep your mind, heart, and spirit open to the magic and the miracles that are waiting for you, because they are there.

If you enjoy reading memoirs and biographies, maybe you'd enjoy another book: I didn't write it; my mother did, but I'm your humble editor. The book is a collection of letters she wrote to her family back home while she and her family – husband and three young children – spent about a year and a half in France during the years 1959 and 1960.

Here's the introduction from *Letters From Paris,* by Linnie Farrell Southard, edited by DeMar Southard, available in all electronic formats and hopefully, by the time you read this, in paper.

Letters From Paris

By Linnie Farrell Southard, edited by DeMar Southard

My father, Donald Gene Southard, was born in Miami, Texas in 1930. My mother, Linnie Farrell Holly, was born two years later in Stacy, Texas, a town which no longer exists. They met near the end of my father's enlistment in the U.S. Navy as a sonarman serving aboard the destroyer USS Radford during the Korean War. When his enlistment ended in 1950 he returned to Texas and went to work for The Electric Supply Company in Pampa, a small town at that time in the Northern Panhandle.

I can't count all the places my mother lived between Stacy and Pampa, Texas. She and her family of four – my grandmother, "Mother Bee," her sister, Yoby, and brother, Guy – lived a gypsy lifestyle during the depression and war years and lived in no less than twenty towns in probably a dozen states during that time. When my mother graduated from high school, after attending countless schools whenever and wherever she happened to live, she did so early and with honors. I edited neither grammar nor spelling in her letters reprinted here – everything is exactly as she wrote. I believe few high school graduates of the twenty-first century could write so well.

My father and mother married in 1952. After the wedding the two of them decided to head for Seattle, Washington to seek better opportunities. But running into a snow storm on the way there, and being stuck in California, they decided to take the next best option and headed for, of all destinations, Florida. As my mother would say, "Ha!" They arrived in West Palm Beach and through a friend from his Navy days, my father found employment with another electric company as a lineman. A little time in the swamp land of Florida is all it took to discover a deep seated hatred of the heat and humidity and chiggers and other crawly things that a lineman has to live with in the southern part of that state. A little bit of that life was enough to convince my mother and father that Florida was not a good place to live and they returned, now with my sister, Sherma Layne, who was born in 1953, to Texas to again work for The Electric Supply Company.

The path to a better career seemed to be more education in computers and electronics, so my father began taking a correspondence course from a school in Washington, D.C. Taking a correspondence course and studying at night after work, proved to be difficult living a block from my mother's parents and close to many other relatives. In Texas, Southern cultural roots run deep and Southern society is extremely friendly and neighborly. Few nights passed without a lengthy visit from a friend or relative, or both, and making sufficient progress in a correspondence course at night proved to be impossible. My parents decided the best thing to do would be to move to Washington, D.C., the home base of the correspondence school, and for my father to go to school full time there as a regular student. Just "git 'er done," as they say.

Thus my father, mother, and sister moved to Washington, D.C., where not only did my father complete the course in computers and electronics, but my brother, Don Marion was born in 1955.

At about the time my father completed his degree, the Burroughs Corporation was recruiting new employees at the school and he was hired for the unheard of sum of $455 per month. My parents had finally struck it rich and life was good! Burroughs transferred my family to California, where I was born in 1957, then to Bartlesville, Oklahoma, then to Midland, Texas, and finally to France as part of a small team to install a computer system for a service bureau called Compta Technic.

Our family of five — Mother, Daddy, Sherma Layne, Don Marion and I — moved to France to begin one of those adventures that may not have seemed so wonderful while we were in it, but turned out to be life changing and a watershed for the little community we call our family.

I hope you enjoy reading the daily experiences of my family in France, recorded ninety-nine percent by my mother, <u>Linnie Farrell, to whom this book is lovingly dedicated.</u>